*The reader,
the library
and the book*

The reader, the library and the book

selected papers 1949-1970

A W McCLELLAN

College of Librarianship Wales
formerly Director of Tottenham Libraries & Museum

CLIVE BINGLEY  LONDON

FIRST PUBLISHED IN A COLLECTED EDITION 1973
BY CLIVE BINGLEY LTD 16 PEMBRIDGE ROAD LONDON W11
SET IN 10 ON 12 POINT LINOTYPE PLANTIN
AND PRINTED IN THE UK BY THE CENTRAL PRESS (ABERDEEN) LTD
COPYRIGHT © A W MCCLELLAN 1973
ALL RIGHTS RESERVED
0 85157 164 6

Contents

1*

Acknowledgements

I wish to thank the following editors and publishers for permission to reproduce the undermentioned material:

The Library Association, London and Home Counties Branch for the paper, *The social survey and reading* (1953). The *Library Association record* for the papers, *New concepts of service* (1956), *What are we up to?* (1962), *The organisation of a library for subject specialisation* (1955) and *Library developments affecting the book trade* (1967). The Polytechnic of North London, Department of Librarianship for the paper, *Professional work for professional librarians* (1958). The Editor *New library world* for the paper, *Accessibility and other problems of book provision* (1962) and for parts of the following articles, *A new policy or a new approach?* (1949), *Reading as communication* (1949) and ' *Service in depth* ' (1950).

My thanks are also due to those of my colleagues at the College of Librarianship Wales who encouraged me to publish the material in this book.

A special debt of gratitude is due to my former colleagues of the Tottenham Public Libraries who contributed so much to my thinking on library problems by way of criticism and discussion, and by co-operation in its implementation in a practical library situation.

College of Librarianship Wales   A W MCCLELLAN
March 1973

Introduction

THE increasing application of management techniques to the administration of local authority services, including the use of independent teams to assess the effectiveness of the use of resources, obliges the librarian to be clear as to his objectives and to be in a position to justify *his* use of resources. A parallel trend towards the creation of fewer and larger local government units and consequently larger library systems, further obliges the librarian to practise substantial delegation of his principal functions to subordinate professional staff. Nevertheless, he will continue to bear ultimate responsibility, and so will need to develop ways of retaining effective control of the library's activities and, in particular, its bookstock, without cramping the style of his professional specialists.

These developments have prompted librarians to re-examine the assumptions which, hitherto, they have relied upon to justify their activities, and to look to principles of management for ways to improve their methods and organisations. On a longer view a possibly more disturbing development is the technical progress in mass communications through sophisticated audio-visual systems and in computer-based information retrieval systems. Will they have a mutative effect on the roles of the book and the library?

If the problems arising from these developments are now attracting considerable attention, this is not to say that, in lesser or greater degree, they have not been with us for a long time. They have, and the following papers embody some of the thinking about them and the practical implications of that thinking which one librarian found it necessary to engage in over the greater part of a professional life. Most of these papers represent stages in a long process of dissatisfaction with criteria and practice leading to fresh thinking, leading to modifications in criteria and practice and so on. The result, occasionally, is some repetitiveness or overlapping, as for example may be noted in the description of a stock control system in paper 7 'Accessibility and other problems of book provision', which is superseded by a more sophisticated version described in paper 8, 'Systematic stock control in public libraries'. The contrast, however, serves to illustrate the way in which thinking about that particular problem evolved.

Underlying all the papers are certain unifying themes. Although the principal skill characteristic of the librarian must be his knowledge of books and allied resources—that is to say in the widest sense, his bibliographical skill—this must be applied within a framework formed by the institutional nature of the library and the characteristics of the subject of all his activities, reading and the *use* of books. The key theme is the conviction that purpose, and the objectives which will achieve purpose, must derive from the understanding that the library is part of the total system of communications operating within society, and from the individual and social implications of the reading activity itself. What is the particular contribution of the book as one medium of many, of the library as one channel of many, to the communication system as a whole? What values reside in the reading activity? What are the relationships involved, more especially, with the media of mass communications? How do readers and non-readers behave in relation to reading and libraries? These papers do not pretend to the right answers but offer possible starting points, and always with the practical implications for the library in mind.

Is the concern with reading and the role of the library in the communications system becoming increasingly irrelevant? Is the book and print era coming to an end in the face of the vast increase in non-print communication? There is some evidence that recorded loans from public libraries may be declining. There is renewed concern about the so-called 70 percent of non-users of public libraries. Raymond Williams has averred that the 'control of the means of communication will pass into still fewer hands . . . the range of choice of newspapers, magazines and books will steadily diminish—as a writer's opinion comes to matter less and less and whether he sells to matter more and more'. Does this presage the possibility that libraries' sources for worthwhile books will cease?

That these questions can be asked and that answers are still awaited reinforces the belief that understanding of the roles of readers and libraries remains inadequate. Consider the ambivalent and uncertain attitude of librarians to recorded loans from libraries. There is a whole range of factors which singly or in various combinations can affect the recorded number of loans. Some are local and others are national in nature. The mere alteration of loan periods within a library system will affect the record of loans. The most prolific reading group in the community, the young adult, has been diverted from the public library for temporary periods in places of higher education to an increasing extent. We know that reading falls off with age and the proportion of elderly people in the population is rising. Another high-potential reading group, the middle-class, is moving away from the urban areas. Even a change from fiction to non-fiction reading, sometimes brought about by deliberate policy of encouraging what is regarded as more desirable literature, will reduce the number of recorded loans—on average a non-fiction book will be borrowed for twice as long as a novel. There is the impact of widespread viewing of colour television which is accelerating and will become more or less universal in due course. Its initial impact is without doubt considerable. It will affect reading; but permanently?

There is only one book written by an English librarian specifically on reading—Harold Bonny's *Reading: an historical and psychological study* (Philip, 1939). Is it to be wondered at that so many questions relating to readers and reading remain without even partial answers.

But to conclude on a positive note, let Alex Comfort speak: 'The growing points of social progress are not in Westminster or Moscow, but in study and research . . . through the growth of ideas and attitudes'.

Reading has something to do with that.

1: *The social survey and reading*

PROFESSOR Norbert Weiner[1] has suggested that the present century might be described as the century of communication. Certainly the last fifty years have witnessed an unprecedented growth in all forms of communication among which the radio, television, the cinema, newspapers and magazines appear to rival the much older habit of book-reading. Increasing interest has been aroused, therefore, in the extent of book-reading and in its relation to the other forms of so-called mass-media. One form which this interest has taken has been the social survey of the book-reading habit.

The social survey as a method of studying reading behaviour has been the subject of misunderstanding. 'A social survey is a process by which quantitative facts are collected about the social aspects of a community's composition and activities . . . it is essentially a *method* of collecting facts; the limiting adjective " social " indicates that the information assembled describes the way people live as social beings, that is, as parts of a group . . .'.[10] Thus, Mark Abrams in his excellent book on the social survey. He goes on to show that this method of collecting facts was discovered and developed by British pioneers like Booth, Rowntree and Bowley. These three, between them, developed the essential features of the social survey; the collection of factual information in direct interviews with the people being studied, the application of precise quantitative definitions to loose conceptions such as poverty and the collection of material from a representative cross section instead of from the whole population. The information obtained from a representative sample scientifically selected has been shown to be true, within very close limits, for the population as a whole. The main likely source of error in the social survey method is in the interview itself. Both the form in which questions are put and the bias of the interviewer may distort the information obtained. Experienced investigators, however, are fully aware of these difficulties and have developed a number of ways to minimise their effects.

The social survey should not be confused with the ' public opinion poll '. Although the sampling technique is common to both, their objectives are different. The public opinion poll is concerned with the *opinions* of the interviewees and usually in order to obtain an estimate of how people will react to some public question. The social survey is concerned primarily with what people actually do or what are the actual circumstances in which people do things. This distinction becomes particularly important when it is appreciated that the information obtained from a sample group, is, strictly speaking, only true at the time the sample is interviewed. A further survey undertaken even at a short interval may yield quite different results. This is likely to be specially so when the object is the assessment of opinion. It also emphasises the value of comparing surveys made at different times and in different areas if trends in behaviour are to be accurately assessed.

The interpretation of reading surveys is very much dependent on a knowledge of other aspects of reading such as the nature of the reading process, the social and personal implications of reading, and the relation of reading to the whole field of human communication. For example, the activity of communication is in itself important to the individual and to the community; the characteristics of the groups which control the various forms of communication may also be significant; book-reading possesses characteristics which make it significantly different from radio-listening and other forms of so-called mass-media. The lack of co-ordinated work on the psychology and sociology of reading explains, possibly, why the practical value of the social survey on reading is not always apparent.

The value of the social survey is sometimes deprecated because of a misunderstanding of its purpose or through fear of its consequences. In the case of reading surveys it has been said that they should not determine libraries' policies. It is also said that they may provide ammunition for those who are opposed to the development of libraries. Obviously a survey should not determine policy. The purpose of a survey can only be to provide a factual description of the situation which policy has to deal with. For instance, a survey may indicate the critical distance from a library service point beyond which most readers will not bother to visit the library. That finding merely presents information. What is done about it, if anything, is a matter of policy for the library service concerned. If policy is, to provide reasonably equal access to library facilities to all the citizens, the survey finding indicates the maximum distance required between library service points. If, however, policy is concerned with attracting what some might describe as the best readers to one service point, the survey findings will indicate approximately the number of such readers who may be expected to travel to a central service point in spite of the distances involved. In the matter of public taste the BBC Listener Research organisation illustrates the answers to both points. It is quite certain that the BBC doesn't permit the findings of Listener Research to determine policy. Listener Research provides the BBC with an instrument for discovering some of the factors which must be taken into account if the policy already determined upon is to succeed. The BBC also keeps to itself the findings of Listener Research, possibly because some of them could be misapplied. The question of what findings from a survey should be published is a matter for the sponsors of the survey and will depend on its purpose. As a general principle, however, it is doubtful whether the suppression of factual information even if of an inconvenient nature is of advantage to the suppressor. The proper function of the survey is to provide an independent and objective description of the behaviour of groups of people in relation to particular activities and situations. In the language of the communications engineer it is a form of feed back enabling the organisation or system concerned to modify its behaviour the better to achieve its own particular policy or function.

As early as 1926 a committee appointed jointly by the American Library Association and the American Association for Adult Education was set up to gather the available facts about adult reading and to obtain additional facts by direct investigation. With the publication of *The reading interests and habits of adults*[2] by W S Gray and Ruth Munroe in 1929 there followed a number of interesting investigations into the reading habits of Americans. In general, however, these investigations were limited to special or localised groups of people or again, to special aspects of reading. In 1946 the Book Manufacturers' Institute, New York, published the results of a national survey of reading and book buying habits under the title *People and Books*[3] by Link and Hopf. Among the reports prepared for the American Public Library Inquiry were two which dealt directly with the reading-habit. *The library's public*[4] by Bernard Berelsen and Lester Asheim included the findings of the national survey carried out by the Survey Research Center of the University of Michigan and an analysis of all the studies of library book use and users published since 1930. In *The effects of mass media*[5] Joseph T Klapper analysed the extant literature on the following; the impact of mass media upon public taste; the comparative effects of the various media of communication; the functions and effects of escapistic communication; mass-media and persuasion.

The studies referred to relate solely to the United States of America and must, therefore, be treated with caution so far as any application to conditions here is concerned. No national survey has been published in this country, but there are available British surveys which make some contribution to the subject and the findings of which might be compared usefully with those of the American material. Mass-Observation carried out a private survey of the 'book-behaviour' of the British people in 1942.[6] Although conditions were abnormal at that time, the survey is the only one known to have attempted a national picture. Mass-Observation also carried out a survey in the Borough of Tottenham in 1946, a summary of which was published under the title *Reading in Tottenham*.[7] The Division of Research Techniques, London School of Economics and Political Science carried out a survey published as *Reading habits in three London boroughs*.[8] This survey was undertaken in 1950 and fortunately included the Borough of Tottenham as one of the boroughs surveyed, thus making possible a comparison with the Mass-Observation survey of 1946 in the same borough. The British Institute of Public Opinion[9] at approximately yearly intervals since the war, has asked questions relating to books being currently read by people representative of the population as a whole. The information so obtained is limited and does not constitute a complete social survey of the reading habit, but it has the advantage of being nationally representative. These British sources taken together enable a number of useful comparisons to be made with the more complete American material.

In attempting comparisons between the different surveys numerous difficulties are encountered. The analysis of results by the categories of age, sex, education and socio-economic status is common to them all but the definitions of the categories used varies from survey to survey. The surveys use age-groupings which do not coincide. Educational groups are less disparate but national differences occur. The category of socio-economic status is the most difficult of all in this respect, one survey using arbitrarily defined income levels, another, an undisclosed definition of social status and another, perhaps, a series of occupational groups. Difficulty occurs too in the definition of what constitutes a book reader. Nevertheless the categories are very broadly similar in most cases and permit some legitimate comparisons to be made.

In the confines of a paper it is not possible to examine many of the comparable findings. It is proposed to examine, therefore, only a few groups of questions such as the incidence of book reading by age, sex, education and socio-economic status; how book-readers appear to differ from non-readers, and some factors in readers' selection and choice of books.

How many people are active or regular readers of books? The British Institute of Public Opinion has asked the question ' Do you happen to be a book reader at the moment? ' at regular intervals since 1946. About 50 percent of the adult population has answered ' yes ' to this question. Over a period of five years, the tendency has been for the number to increase to rather more than 50 percent. Other British surveys confirm this figure. The American survey by Link and Hopf shows the number of ' active readers ' as 50 percent of the adult population. The number of people who admit to never reading a book at all is about 40 percent, leaving a marginal group of 10 percent who may be described as inactive or intermittent readers.

There does not appear to be any significant difference between the sexes in the proportions who are active readers, whether here or in America. Significant differences are indicated in all surveys, however, for age, education and socio-economic status. Those for educational level are the most marked. The degree to which groups at various educational levels differ is well illustrated in the following tabulation:

Reading habits in three London boroughs (1950)[8]

Educational level:	Elementary	Central	Secondary
Percent of respondents ever reading books	51	$75\frac{1}{2}$	$85\frac{1}{2}$

Reading in Tottenham (1946)[7]

	Elementary		Secondary
Percent Regular users of books	49	—	71

People and Books (1945—USA)[3]

	Grade school	High school	College
Percent Active readers of books	25	51	71

The persistence of these contrasts in the relationship of reading to educational levels is to be noted in all surveys and studies on reading. It would be unwise, however, to assume that the extent of book-reading in any group is a direct consequence of a particular level of education. It is much more likely that the level of education masks a deeper factor. The close correlation between what is known as general mental ability or, general intelligence (factor g), and ability to read is indicated by many studies in educational psychology, eg Schonell[11] and *Studies in reading*.[12] It would appear that educational level reflects this factor and other, possibly cultural factors, which, taken together, affect the propensity to reading.

The contrast between the youngest and oldest age-groups is also strongly marked, eg

	Age groups—percent users of books
Reading in Tottenham[7]	16-20, 79; 21-40, 58; 41 or over, 44
Reading habits in three London boroughs[8]	Under 30 years—$75\frac{1}{2}$; 50 or over, 41
People and books[3]	15-19 years, 77; 20-29 years, 59; 50-59 years, 38

It is also interesting to note that use of the public library is about twice as high among the adolescent group as among any other age group. There is little doubt that the educational factor is partly reflected in the age-group contrasts. Analysing the educational composition of the sample reported in *Reading habits in three London boroughs*[8] it is found that of the under 30 age group 68 percent had received elementary schooling only, while of the over 50 age group 92 percent had received elementary schooling only. Nevertheless, with increasing responsibilities and decreasing leisure the habit of reading suffers. The effect of marriage for example, is well brought out in the Tottenham survey.[7]

The contrast in the use of books by groups at different socio-economic levels is also significant eg,

Reading in Tottenham[7] percentage of regular book users in middle class is 92; skilled working class, 60; unskilled working class, 42.

People and books[3] percentage of active readers in income groups is, upper, 64; middle, 48; lower 36.

Link and Hopf in *People and books,* show that there is a close correlation between income level and education, and that the educational level is the more important factor in the differences in the use of books although, cultural variations and variations in leisure available at different socio-economic levels have their effect as well.

The surveys do indicate quite clearly that educational level (or possibly level of general mental ability) is the decisive factor in the habit of using books. Youth, and improved socio-economic status are secondary but important favourable factors.

Despite the influence of education and social status there are substantial numbers of active book readers in all groups in the community. Are there then any significant distinctions between the book-readers and the non-readers as such? To this question all the surveys which have dealt with it give much the same answers. Campbell and Metzner[13] in their survey prepared for the Public Library Inquiry find that ' the book reading public appears to be one intensely interested in all forms and avenues of communication—they not only read more, but they listen more and they see more . . .'. People who read books, particularly the heavy consumers of books, are more likely to read both newspapers and magazines than those who read no books. Berelson[4] also quotes from an investigation which shows that the book-readers are among the more critically minded persons in the community. They are particularly critical of the communication media available.

An especially marked characteristic of book readers in general is their greater interest in all kinds of activities other than reading. The diagram on page 18 illustrates graphically the greater degree of interest shown by book-readers as compared with non-readers in a wide range of activities. The gap between the two graph curves is consistent throughout the range, except in the cases of ' pools ', ' pubs ' and horse and dog racing, where the non-readers show a greater interest.

The graph was compiled from information available in one of the field reports made by Mass-Observation in preparation of their publication *The press and the people*. The findings shown are fully confirmed by cross-checking questions used in the survey. The following table compiled from the same source is also included to show where the differences between the book-readers and the non-readers are most apparent. The activities are ranked in order of the greatest difference.

Interests ranked to show those in which interviewees who indicated that they were *very interested in reading* differed most as compared with interviewees who expressed themselves as *not interested in reading*

Activity in which great interest is expressed	Percentage greater interest shown by interviewees very interested in reading
1 Music (concert)	+208
2 Foreign affairs	+143
3 Politics	+114
4 Crime	+ 99

5	Social work	+ 92
6	Dancing	+ 90
7	Recreation	+ 66
8	Games	+ 59
9	Clubs	+ 54
10	Films	+ 47
11	Religion	+ 33
12	Radio	+ 15
13	Gardening	+ 13
14	Pools	− 20
15	Dogs (racing)	− 25
16	Horses (racing)	− 28
17	Pubs	− 31

A sidelight on this question of interests is to be noted in a survey undertaken by A M Carr-Saunders, Hermann Mornleim and E C Rhodes in 1938[15] into the leisure interests of 1,000 juvenile delinquents and a central group of matched non-delinquents. It was found that in the London area 56·2 percent of the delinquents had no leisure interests, as against 15·2 percent of the non-delinquents, and in the provincial towns the respective figures were 35·5 percent and 10·3 percent. The same survey reported some considerable differences in reading interests as between the delinquents and non-delinquents.

Campbell and Metzner[13] quote a Survey Research Centre Study, *Interest, information and attitudes in the field of world affairs* (November 1949) and comment: ' These and other interrelations support the hypothesis that there is a general " activity pattern ", that high rank in one sphere of activity tends to be related to high rank in another, within limits '.

The greater interest shown in other activities by book-readers may be considered to reflect only the influence of educational level or degree of general mental ability. Link and Hopf,[3] who are very conscious of this influence, show, however, that there is an independent relationship between interest in other activities and the reading of books. An analysis of their findings indicates that the active readers express greater interest in other activities than do the non-readers at the same educational level.

The high correlation between book reading and interest in other activities bears on the controversial question as to whether other forms of communication, in particular in recent years, television, are serious

18

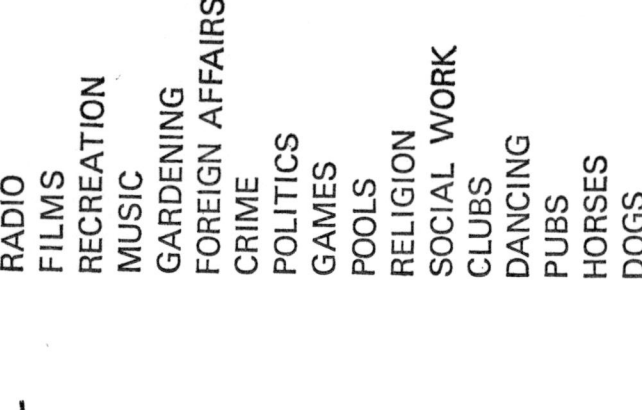

—— indicates habitual readers interested in these activities

– – – indicates non–habitual readers interested in these activities

FIGURE I

competitors to reading. American and British investigations suggest that each media acts as an ' energising agent ' in relation to the others. In other words, the active, intelligent members of the community use all forms of communication to a much greater extent than do the less intelligent. Radio and possibly television reach all groups and levels to roughly the same extent. Radio appears to have the effect of scanning the whole spectrum of interests to which the individual is predisposed and energising some of them into greater activity. As Klapper[5] reports, ' reading stimulation was more common among the heavier readers than the light readers, radio rarely, if ever, operating in a vacuum of reading interest '. That is to say, radio does not create interests, but, owing to its simple accessibility and its availability at the opportune time, stimulates an existing predisposition and matures its development. The Link and Hopf[3] survey finds that the reading of books is not necessarily a substitute for other activities, but a supplement to them.

What influences people to choose particular books? Unfortunately the social survey material at present available offers little firm information on this aspect of the reading habit. Klapper[5] concludes from a study of a number of investigations among radio listeners, film-goers and readers, that people seek out material of their own cultural level and avoid or reject other material. This self-selective process appears to render the individual immune from influences which do not fit his personality pattern, or, more simply, his predispositions. A detailed examination of studies concerned with the relationships of the audiences to the various media shows that there are a number of important qualifications to such a statement, as for example when the media is dealing with factors outside the usual experience of the audience, but, in general, it is probably correct. Its implications are certainly interesting, especially for example in considering the question of the affects of reading on taste and it is tempting to enlarge upon it. Klapper[5] examines many investigations into the affects of the various media on ' taste ' and will repay reading.

Some attempts have been made to discover the practical ways in which people choose their reading. The Mass-Observation Survey in 1942[6] dealt at some length with the factors of choice and placed them in the following order of importance :

Author
Personal recommendation
' Book looked good '

Special interest in subject
Reviews
Random choice
Title, etc.

The order of importance, however, was shown to vary considerably with the different social and educational levels. Personal recommendation was an important factor in all groups, reviews on the other hand were of real importance only in the highest social and educational levels. The actual proportions of the groups influenced by reviews is of interest in view of the extensive reviewing of books which takes place. By social class the figures given are:

Upper and middle class	25 percent
Lower middle and upper working class	11 percent
Unskilled working class	2 percent.

The contrast for educational levels is even more marked:

Those with college education	30 percent
Those with secondary education	18 percent
Those with elementary education	1 percent.

The same survey showed that when reviews were influential in the selection of books, there was a sex difference in the attitude to reviews. On the whole women were much less critical of reviews than men. Men tended to read between the lines and evaluated them in the light of previous reviews from the same source to a greater extent.

The relative unimportance of reviews as a *direct* factor of choice is reinforced by a number of non-British sources. L N Schücking in his *Sociology of literary taste* (Kegan Paul, 1944) reports experiments carried out by two large German publishing firms. Each showed that a large percentage of purchasers had bought books on the strength of personal recommendation. In respect of one particular book, while 160 copies had been bought on the strength of a review, no fewer than 391 purchases were due to personal recommendation.

By a slight re-arrangement of the categories into which the findings are analysed it is possible to include for comparison the results of two American surveys.

Link and Hopf[3]	percent
Interest in subject etc	39
Recommendations	31
*Advertising and reviews	15

* This heading includes also such factors as 'heard about book on

radio ', ' saw movie and wanted to read the book ', and illustrates the point made earlier that the various media act as ' energising agents ' for each other.

City of Los Angeles[14]	percent
Own interests (interest in author, subject or in books examined)	47
Impersonal suggestions (reviews, advertisements, book clubs, movies)	32
Personal recommendation	27

The Mass-Observation Survey[6] dealt with an aspect of choice which no other survey appears to have done, namely, the effect of the actual make-up and appearance of the book. Although this factor operated along with all the other factors of choice the survey indicated clearly that ' the general feel and look of the book is most often associated with the least informed and the least enthusiastic readers '.

Under the heading ' the general feel and look of the book ' this survey examined in detail preferences relating to such aspects as : book covers and colours; size of book; typography; the number of pages in a book; cleanliness of book; illustrations etc. Among other things it appears that blue is much the most popular colour throughout the country and especially among women !

The Los Angeles survey is purely local in character, so that the information relating to the choosing of books is, unfortunately, inadequate to justify any but tentative conclusions. So far as it goes, however, it suggests that the heavy book users, the higher social and educational groups, are less influenced by arbitrary factors, that reviews have a very limited direct influence and, in the case of non-fiction books, recommendation and random choice are much less extensive than is the case in the selection of fiction.

It has been possible to examine but a few of the questions dealt with by the reading surveys; sufficient it is hoped, however, to indicate the nature of these investigations and to stimulate further interest in them. Many other aspects of the reading habit could have been mentioned such as the factors which appear to inhibit reading, the effects of accessibility both geographical and psychological and the particular characteristics of book-reading as a distinct medium of communication. The various surveys have something to say on all these and similar questions.

Frequently, the first reaction to the subject of reading surveys is one of doubt as to their practical utility, or it may be said that most experienced librarians are already aware of the factors revealed in them. To a degree these are legitimate criticisms. A survey may not convey much of immediate practical value to a particular library service, although it is seldom completely so. It is obvious, too, that some librarians with many years of keen application to their job will have quite shrewd ideas of the factors at work so far as reading is concerned. Even so, it does involve many years of experience and the surveys can help the less experienced librarian to reduce the time required. But even the experienced librarian is seldom able to judge accurately the weight of the many and complex factors involved. In my own libraries I found that certain subjects which the survey had shown to be high up on the list of interests indicated by the readers of the area were very poorly represented in the libraries' book stock. It is possible that through the natural tendency of any librarian to be guided by the expressed interests of those who use his library, his bookstocks come to represent a range of interests which coincides less and less with the range of interests of the whole of the active reading group in the service area. Those readers who find the bookstocks inadequate and bring the inadequacy to the attention of the librarian are in the minority; the majority just cease to use the library. From discussions with colleagues about the findings of various surveys it is clear that in numerous ways they can act as a corrective to the empirical judgement of the practising librarian.

But it is not the possibilities of immediate practical application in which the greatest value is to be found. Granted that reading as an activity is a major concern of the public librarian, then the more he knows about it and the part it plays in the life of the community, the better will public libraries fulfil their task. The social survey enlarges our perception of the nature of reading, stimulates questions which would not otherwise be asked, and by drawing out the common characteristics of readers within the many groupings into which they fall permits a greater concentration on those characteristics in which the individual reader differs from those in his group. If there is one principal lesson of immediate value to be learned from a study of reading surveys, it is that the public library needs to cater, not for a simple majority of readers, but for the greatest possible number of minorities.

1 Wiener, Norbert: *Cybernetics; or control and communication in the animal and the machine.* The Technology Press, John Wiley & Sons Inc, New York, 1949. Chapman & Hall, 1949.

2 Gray, William S and Munroe, Ruth: *Reading interests and habits of adults.* Macmillan, New York and London, 1929.

3 Link, Henry C and Hopf, Harry Arthur: *People and books: a study of reading and book-buying habits.* Book Industry Committee, Book Manufacturers' Institute, New York, 1946.

4 Berelson, Bernard and Asheim, Lester: *The library's public [a report of The Public Library Inquiry].* Columbia University Press, New York, 1949. OUP, 1949.

5 Klapper, Joseph T: *The effects of mass-media; a report to the Director of The Public Library Inquiry, Bureau of Applied Social Research.* Columbia University, New York, 1949.

6 *Books and the public: a private report* made by Mass-Observation, 1943.

7 *Reading in Tottenham: a report on a survey carried out by Mass-Observation on behalf of the Tottenham Borough Council* [in 1946]. Borough of Tottenham, 1952.

8 Stuart, A: 'Reading habits in three London boroughs'. *Journal of documentation,* vol 8, no 1, March 1952, pp 33-49.

9 British Institute of Public Opinion: private papers.

10 Abrams, Mark A: *Social surveys and social action.* Heinemann, 1951.

11 Schonell, Fred J: *The psychology and teaching of reading.* Oliver & Boyd, 1949.

12 *Studies in reading, volume 1* [Publications of the Scottish Council for Research in Education xxvi]. University of London Press, 1949.

13 Campbell, Angus and Metzner, Charles A: *Public use of the library and other sources of information.* University of Michigan, Institute for Social Research, Ann Arbor, Michigan, 1950. [A report prepared for the Public Library Inquiry.]

14 Los Angeles, City of. Bureau of Budget and Efficiency: *Organisation, administration and management of the Los Angeles Public Library: vol 1, General service factors.* City of Los Angeles, 1948.

15 Saunders, A M Carr (and others): *Young offenders: an enquiry into juvenile delinquency.* Cambridge University Press, 1943.

2: *The readership survey and the public library*

INVESTIGATIONS into the reading activities of people and into related fields are now sufficiently numerous to justify drawing a number of conclusions from them. It would be true to say that the quality and scope of the investigations have varied considerably; the reliability of particular investigations could be questioned; nevertheless, when considered together, a number of common factors and trends are evident. An examination of these in the light of their bearing on the public library service may reveal whether they have any useful application, the utility or otherwise of more readership surveys and, possibly, whether there are aspects of reading as an activity which it would be valuable to have investigated more closely, or with more refined methods than the readership surveys have so far attempted or employed.

The factors and trends related to reading established so far concern several important aspects of public library provision. These may be stated as: the role of the public library and the purposes it serves; standards of library provision; and, the relationships of librarian, reader and books.

Joseph Trenaman[1] undertook a survey which, although not primarily concerned with reading, had as he says ‘ as part of its objective ’ an inquiry into people's attitudes to educational opportunities and the way their varying sources of ideas continue to influence them. He found that the influence of libraries emerged as a potent and independent force; that the real work of deepening and disciplining the minds of the educationally undeveloped must largely fall to the public library. He concluded that libraries are, therefore, of unique social importance, for they stand midway between the beginnings of learning and its mature expression!

The survey revealed, as is confirmed by other investigations, that the population falls into two broad categories: those who have a positive attitude towards learning in its broadest sense, and those whose attitude is negative. The latter, possibly due to a deep-seated antipathy to what is associated with the ‘ top ’ in society, tend to reject formal educational opportunities. Significantly it was found that about one third of the members of public and subscription libraries were in this negative or resistant group.

The existence of a ' cultural gap ' in society is becoming clearer, and, paradoxically, the effect of expanding facilities for education is to widen the gap. It is possible that there may develop in place of the ' two nations ' rich and poor, ' two nations ' of the cultured and the uncultured. The public library therefore not only has an educational role for the more positive group, but perhaps an even more important one in bridging the ' cultural gap '.

All investigations indicate that the use of libraries is much higher proportionately among the better educated, but that quantitatively the number of the poorer educated using libraries is as great if not greater. The attitude of the public library to this group, constituting as it does nearly one half of the population, can be decisive in its social effects.

Book readers show a greater interest in other activities and tend to be the more active and alert citizens. It has been shown that there is an independent relationship between interest in other activities and the reading of books. The active readers express greater interest in other activities than do the non-readers at the same educational level. So that the public library not only plays an educational role, but through its widespread provision of books stimulates a greater participation of people in the work and activities of society.

The part which the public library plays in providing recreational reading is one which has inspired little investigation. Yet it is a part which arouses a good deal of controversy, an indication perhaps that it is a subject about which there is more opinion than fact. It is a part too about which clarity of thinking is marred by a widespread puritanical reaction which tends to assume that any activity prompted by a desire for pleasure, or undertaken solely as an indulgence, is in some way immoral or wasteful. The consideration that whatever the motive for an activity it may yet have useful values for individuals or society is lost. Or, if it is granted that there may be some residual value in such motivated activity, it is dismissed on the assumption that a more seriously motivated activity is ipso facto of more value. A great deal of reading is motivated by the need for relaxation, or for a sedative for the stress which arises in a complex technological society. A psychologist, T T Paterson,[2] has suggested on statistical evidence the hypothesis that industrial phenomena such as accidents, absenteeism and strike intensity are conditioned by social environment. He holds ' that owing to a tendency to preserve social equilibrium (a conservative tendency to be seen in all cultures), continuous adjustment to change in environment is prevented. As a result the stresses set up by conflict between a pre-existing value-system and that for a new environment will reach a point (. . .) where the stress will show itself in various forms. . . . In the broad national sense these will be seen in those phenomena I have mentioned, and also in psychosomatic conditions and forms of delinquency.' In a letter to me he says, ' The social stress which brings about these other phenomena will also set up a demand for reading among some individuals, and specifically for reading of certain types of literature, not only " escapist " in the usual sense but also either as a sedative for the stress or as a means of solving the problem, a search for meaningfulness '.

There is every indication that the stresses in society are increasing, that with the general raising of educational levels the individual is becoming less conformist while at the same time the pressures for conformity are increasing. The value of reading for therapeutic purposes has already been demonstrated. Is there not a need for research into the place and significance of recreational reading? Other than as a source for rather generalised information the readership survey would not appear to be appropriate to such a field of investigation. It calls for the experience and methods of the psychologist and the sociologist. Some further light could be thrown on this matter, perhaps, as a result of some simple statistical investigations which librarians could undertake. If, for example, a series of sample groups of readers in a number of libraries were taken and their reading noted over a period of two or three years, such questions as the range of their reading and their use of non-recreational reading might be answered. It should not be difficult to devise a test experiment to determine whether or not the provision of recreational literature affects the use of non-recreational literature. There are a number of such possibilities which might help to clear the ground of some prejudice.

Some investigations have probed the sources of people's reading, the relationships existing between books, and other forms of so-called mass communication such as radio, films and the press. These have shed some light on a little recognised role of the public library, namely its function simply as an institution. This role has become significant only as the library has become more or less universal. Because of its extension over the whole of the country and because it is the source for a very large amount of the total reading done, it has far reaching consequences which have little to do with what is read or who reads.

It is characteristic of all mass-media that they depend upon the largest possible audiences and consequently succumb to the expression of ideas and attitudes acceptable to the greatest number. Further, because of their size and costliness their progress has been accompanied by a strong tendency towards monopolisation. On the other hand the publication of books is not subject to these limitations. The economic production of individual books is dependent upon a print of but a few thousands of copies. The purchasing power of libraries is such in total, that while it may not be in itself sufficient to support publication, it has a powerful marginal effect which ensures that many books are published which would not be otherwise. Such information as is available also indicates that the active borrowers are also likely to be purchasers of books. The book trade has in consequence, in the public library service, possibly the greatest free sampling organisation available to any trade, at no expense to itself. It is notable that the sale of books have increased hand in hand with the increase in public library borrowing; for example, publishers' home market turnover annually has increased from £25,750,000 in 1950 to 41,500,000 in 1959.

The public library's role as a widespread institution has at least two important social consequences. Because of its key part in enabling small runs of individual titles to be published and made freely available, it has become almost the only universal means for the distribution of ideas and attitudes of extreme minority appeal. And, because it is the only form of such distribution which is completely free of monopolistic pressures, it affords a guarantee that new minority ideas and attitudes will have the opportunity of an audience. It also helps to ensure that the publishing and book trade retains its highly individual character and is economically able to resist the pressure of monopolistic tendencies within itself.

In the present state of society its institutional role may be of greater significance than its role in the broad educational field. If society is to adapt itself successfully to change, the widespread admission and consideration of fresh ideas and attitudes is vital and is necessary to ensure that change is brought about in an essentially democratic manner. Furthermore, in a society which becomes ever more complex, and where the individual finds himself increasingly regarded as simply part of a group, the urge to individuality and non-conformity needs the fullest support. The individual needs to feel that he is not isolated, that his particular ideas and feelings are echoed in other individuals. For him access to the infinite variety of ideas and attitudes to be found in books is essential. The public library makes this possible.

Regardless, therefore, of what is read through the public library, it has primarily a social role to play. Surveys underline this role and confirm its value as a broad informal educational agency occupying an unique place in reducing the 'cultural gap', in guaranteeing the circulation of ideas and attitudes, in sustaining individuality and in promoting democratic change. It is not, therefore, a part of the so-called 'welfare state', because its function is not, primarily, to help the less fortunate at the expense of the more fortunate. The social consequences of a flourishing public library service are vital to all in society whether they make particular use of the service or not. This is the answer to all attempts to limit the service by erecting financial or other barriers to its completely free and unfettered use by all who are minded to do so. More positively, the more individuals who are drawn to use it, the more benefits follow for all.

A great deal needs to be done by way of investigating what constitute acceptable standards of library provision. Standards need to apply to bookstocks, staffing and density of service points within an area. Evidence from readership surveys suggest some general factors which need to be taken into account.

The importance of educational levels within a population group and, to a lesser extent, proportions of different social classes, as an indication of potential readership within an area are paramount. An associated factor is the degree of accessibility the population has to service points in the area. Local geography and transport facilities will affect this, of course, but the higher educational and social groups will tend to be prepared to travel further for their reading matter in any case, because their interest in reading is stronger. In areas, therefore, with comparatively low education and social levels, there will be a need for a higher density in the distribution of library resources. This will be expressed in the need for more service points per acre and a more popular level of bookstock, larger bookstocks per head and consequently, a greater expenditure per head.

It is necessary, therefore in attempting to devise standards of library provision, or in assessing the major shortcomings of particular services, to take these underlying and pervasive factors into account. The following statistical table, which relates to thirteen library areas in the county of Middlesex, illustrates the pervasiveness of some of

28

these factors. The libraries included in the tabulation were selected solely because the information was conveniently to hand and the area as a whole is an homogeneous one.

Library	% reader-ship classes in popu-lation	Rateable value of domestic property per head popula-tion	Issues per head popula-tion	Expend /head popula-tion on books in d	Service hours per 100 acres	No of staff for each service hour open to public	% fiction in adult stock
I	2	3	4	5	6	7	8
A	85·9	15·2	15·5	31·8	6·30	·150	40
B	84·2	15·2	12·1	25·6	3·70	·208	36
C	84·1	11·8	11·9	30·8	8·80	·168	29
D	83·0	11·6	10·5	23·7	3·10	·157	40
E	81·9	12·3	11·3	23·5	5·76	·125	41
F	81·3	11·1	10·2	16·2	6·50	·163	42
G	80·4	11·0	8·8	17·7	3·47	·155	35
H	77·1	11·4	11·9	29·1	5·95	·217	48
I	76·5	11·1	11·9	25·6	4·33	·245	40
J	75·4	10·8	5·6	13·4	1·70	·161	38
K	75·2	9·8	8·8	19·3	7·13	·176	37
L	74·2	9·2	8·3	20·5	4·80	·160	39
M	74·2	8·9	9·4	25·2	9·70	·171	38

The National Census Tables give information about the proportions of various social classes in each 1000 of the population. They are described as: professional; intermediate; skilled; partly skilled; and unskilled. The first three classes may be regarded as the potential readership, and the value of this, for each area, may be taken as the total of the three classes, expressed as a percentage of the whole five. In the tabulation shown the thirteen libraries are ranked in order of their respective potential readerships calculated in this way. The remaining columns are self-explanatory except for those headed ' Service hours per 100 acres ' and ' No of staff for each service hour '. ' Service hours per 100 acres ' expresses the degree of accessibility the population has to the service points available and is calculated by taking the total number of hours all adult lending libraries are open to the public per week and dividing this by the number of acres comprising the area, multiplied by 100. Thus, the time the service is available, is expressed as a factor of the geographical density of the service. 'The number of staff for each service hour' is obtained by dividing the total number of staff employed by the total number of hours previously mentioned.

It must be appreciated that the tabulation is based on a small sample of library areas only and the correlations may be a little co-incidental. Nevertheless, the relationship shown between 'Hours per head of population', the percentage of 'readership classes in the population' and the 'Rateable value of domestic property per head', are sufficiently striking to suggest the value of undertaking a statistical analysis of a similar character over a much larger number of library areas. Even from this tabulation it would seem possible to select individual libraries and to indicate what might well be their major shortcomings, especially in regard to expenditure on books and accessibility of the service to the particular population.

If it were possible to make a survey designed with a close definition of some of these categories and covering many more libraries, it might well prove possible to extend the analysis to a point which would indicate the kinds of maxima desirable in the provision of bookstocks, staff and degree of accessibility to service points. It must be said, of course, that regional and other differences would almost certainly arise, but these might very well come to light in such a form as to suggest how an overall formula should be modified to take them into account.

It is evident however that readership surveys have provided a number of conclusions which must be taken into account when considering standards of provision.

When one comes to consider the bearing of reading studies on the relationships between librarian, reader and books one does so with a feeling of excitement that at last one may be coming to grips with the day to day job of the librarian. Yet the conclusions one finds are so frequently tantalising in their lack of final concreteness that they compel more questions than they answer.

Joseph Trenaman[1] found that nearly half of those readers who dropped out of using the library were 'learning resistant' and he asks the question 'Is there a steady draining away of readers who cannot find books within their limited level of appreciation?'. If the public library is to play any part in closing the so called 'cultural gap', further investigations are needed to try to ascertain the underlying

30

reasons for the steady dropping out of readers. In such cases the desire to read was present. Is it not desirable that the provision of books at a popular level be considered much more carefully than is the case at present?

Some information has been forthcoming on the effect of reading on taste, notably from Joseph T Klapper.[3] His and other studies suggest that readers are self-selecting, *ie* tend to read or take from their reading only what they can accept; that taste is not easily susceptible to improvement. But tastes can be developed and interests stimulated and deepened. One must remember too that reading is not only a matter of taste but of perception of all kinds. It is possible to be taste-deaf in one sense but perceptive in another.

What is quite certain however, is that the effect of a book cannot be assessed from the book alone, but must be a product dependent upon particular readers of that book. In selecting books then, reader and book must be considered together. It is also certain that reading can stimulate and deepen latent interests and extend those already active. This is a field for further investigations which could be undertaken in libraries. It would be valuable to know whether there are patterns of interests which go together and develop one from another in a way sufficiently consistent to enable booklists to be designed around them. The knowledge of such patterns could greatly help the librarian in advising readers. The investigation could follow such simple lines as noting all the books actually borrowed by a sample group of readers over a period of a number of years. Computer charging systems could be adapted to make this a less than laborious task. The work on the interests of readers has been limited due to the confining of inquiries, either to readers' verbal statements of what they are interested in, or to interests noted at one particular time. It is the understanding of the progressive development of readers' interests which would be of most value, so that any research would need to cover a period of time. If a number of libraries were each to undertake similar inquiries, the resulting information is likely to produce conclusions which could be suitable for general application. Of particular interest would be information which could help determine whether or not a more suitable arrangement of books on library shelves would be desirable than is afforded by current classification schemes—a classification by interests, for example.

Surveys have shown that barriers exist within the library. The general layout of the library can affect the reader. Too many books, or the consciousness of too many books puts off numbers of readers. The proximity and nature of shelving has its effect. There may be an optimum size for a publicly accessible stack area which, if exceeded, may lead to more readers being lost than gained. Such are hinted-at possibilities. These problems may be difficult, but their investigation could produce valuable information affecting design and costs of buildings.

Ronald Staveley[4] has drawn attention to some psychological difficulties in reading. Apart from difficulties arising from vocabulary and structure, this aspect of the subject has received little attention except from the educationist's point of view, which is seldom concerned with adult reading. There are scattered about in the literature of psychology suggestions that are helpful. But what is needed is a study of the processes of reading, the social and psychological factors which affect it from the librarian's point of view.

D V Arnold[5] discusses the problems of communication within the library, particularly with reference to the barriers which may interpose between the librarian and the reader. He touches upon the possibility that the technical functions and apparatus, *eg* the public catalogue, may restrict the relationship between the librarian and the reader. Reading surveys have confirmed that the element of personal introduction ranks high in the reader's choice of books. This is fortunate in that it provides the librarian with the opportunity of assisting the reader to obtain the maximum satisfaction from his reading and reinforces the importance of the personal relationship.

It is paradoxical, but true, that the total effect of studies in reading supports the conclusion that the public library serves an overall and vital social role, but its success in this is directly conditional upon the satisfaction of individual readers' needs. This can be accomplished best if the librarian sees as his most important task the diagnosis of the reader's needs and his potential interests and, out of his expert knowledge of books and bibliography, bring the appropriate books to the attention of the reader. To place the catalogue or the bibliography before the reader and to say to him ' There it is, you'll find what you want in that ', is somewhat as if the doctor places the *Materia medica* before his patient with a similar remark.

The deeper one penetrates into the subject of the reader, books and libraries, the more one is inclined to the conclusion that the librarian must adopt the role of consultant. In the future it will be necessary for the librarian in the public library to specialise in narrower fields of literature and to acquire the status of consultant in his relations with his readers. It must become as common to say 'I shall have to consult my librarian' as it is to say 'I shall have to consult my doctor'.

Upon the individual librarian will fall the demand for a more intensive knowledge of the books and literature he is handling, and the know-how to appraise the requirements of readers. The demand upon the public library will be for considerably increased professional staffs, both to enable books to be more closely examined before purchase, and to provide for the intensification and extension of individual service to readers. In these respects we could not do better than note the example of the library services of two major countries, Germany and Russia.

In Germany, professional staffs devote far more attention to the examination of books submitted for purchase than is ever possible in this country; their staffs are correspondingly twice as large. In Russia the emphasis is upon personal attention to individual readers. Whatever motive may be attributed to this emphasis, the fact is that the number of professional staffs engaged in this way is phenomenal as compared with the number here. Each of these countries has appreciated the importance of at least one of the requirements. We must combine the two.

The surveys to date have only touched the fringe of the subject; other possibilities have been indicated. Further studies in this field, not necessarily of the conventional reader-survey type, are essential if the maximum use of resources is to be applied to the accomplishment of the social objectives and the individual satisfactions which are the parallel and inseparable aims of the public library service.

REFERENCES

1 Trenaman, Joseph: 'Libraries as a social force', *Proceedings of the Annual Conference*. Library Association, 1958.

2 Paterson, T T: 'The theory of the social threshold', *The sociological review* vol XLII, section 3, 1960, pp 53-60.

3 Klapper, Joseph T: *The effects of mass media ... Public Library Inquiry*. Columbia University, New York, 1949.

4 Staveley, Ronald: *Notes on some problems in reading*. University of London School of Librarianship & Archives Occasional Publications no 4. University College, 1954.

5 Arnold, D V: *Libraries: some problems in communication*. University of London School of Librarianship & Archives Occasional Publications no 5. University College, 1954.

3: *The reader-centred library*

AS OF 1949-50, the growth and establishment of a field of study devoted exclusively to principles of administration (management) which may be applied to all types of activity and organisation, had been largely overlooked by librarians. Otherwise, librarians would have appreciated that administration gives *effect* to policy and that policy is a function of government.

The confusion of policy with administration has been confined largely to public librarians. The distinction is usually self-evident to the librarians of specialist, private and other non-public libraries, where their limited purposes are implicit in the nature of the authorities or institutions responsible for their maintenance. The purposes to be served by a general public library are neither obviously implicit nor clearly specified. Nevertheless, the relationship in this respect between the authority and the administrator is the same in each case. If policy is a function of government, it must, in the case of the public library, derive from the nature of the library authority and the librarian as administrator must give effect to it. To say, however, that policy derives from the nature of the library authority requires some clarification. The library authority operates within a framework of legislation and subject to the interests of the community which it serves. Within such a context, therefore, the library authority is charged with ensuring that the activity of the library service shall develop and realise the community values which may be inherent in its medium, the *use* of books and related materials. 'Community' in this sense is not to be confused with the authority itself or with the state, which are but particular associations or organs of the community for particular and different purposes.

Such a policy justifies the taxation of citizens who may not directly benefit from the service provided, and refutes any claim for a direct charge to the user. It also follows that the demands of individuals or groups, whether minorities or majorities, cannot be sole factors in determining provision. The only criterion must be the degree to which community values may be realised, and not only does this require that certain services should be made available to those who may care or take the trouble to use them, but, as with public health and education, there is an obligation on the authority to encourage their widest dissemination.

If the library authority is responsible for the general policy then the librarian as administrator gives effect to it. To do so, however, he must have an understanding of the nature of his medium and, as would be the case in any other field of activity, he must first ascertain what characteristics in his medium are appropriate to policy and how best they may be realised. Only then will he have a basis for planning and organising the means.

The traditional approach has been to place such an emphasis on *books* as the subject of the library's activity that the *actual* subject of this activity has been in danger of being overlooked. The values with which the public library is concerned may only be realised from *books in use,* which implies an emphasis on the reader at least as much as upon the book. It is the process of using books, *ie* reading as an activity, and the behaviour of the reader in relation to the book and the library, which are the librarian's principal concern. Not only is it necessary to know books and readers; the librarian must also seek an understanding of *what happens* when people read and what influences the reader's behaviour towards reading and the library. A study of the reading process involves some reference to the fields of physiology and psychology, from which may be learnt that reading evokes experiences of a similar order to those stimulated by other activities; that reading is not concerned solely with literary, aesthetic or even simply informative values, but with other values too which are vital to the individual's and the community's development. Reading is the public librarian's medium and it needs to be seen as part of the whole field of human activity. Only then will it be possible to elicit the whole range of values potential to the library service. Only then will appropriate criteria of progress be developed. To make a 'mystique' of librarianship is to isolate its theory from the general field of knowledge. An impasse as to fundamental objectives will be overcome when librarianship recognises the true nature of the librarian's medium and maintains a continuous study of its characteristics.

Reading is essentially a means of communication. The author seeks to share an experience with, or to offer information to, the reader. But, as Richards[1] in his *Practical criticism* shows experimentally, the success of the author's attempt is as much dependent upon the reader as upon the author's own writing skill. The experience conveyed in a particular poem is appreciated in varying degrees by different readers. Here the use of the word 'experience' is intended to include all that may be communicated or evoked by the written word.

What are the factors affecting the success of communication by means of the written word? Obviously, the ability of the writer in the use of language is one, but the comprehension of the reader is of major importance. The skill of the writer is of no avail if the reader is lacking in comprehension, for the experience will not be fully shared. The reader's comprehension may be conditioned in a number of ways. Understanding of the language, extent of vocabulary—in other words, the technical ability to read—play a part. Practice in reading tends to improve this factor in comprehension and it is questionable whether the value to be obtained from reading anything at all is sufficiently appreciated. Another factor in comprehension is the sum total of the previous experience and intellectual background of the particular reader. If the experience which the author is trying to convey has no relation to anything in the experience of the reader, comprehension is likely to be difficult. This is exemplified in the well known principle, in teaching, of proceeding from the known to the unknown. Comprehension will also be modified by what can be described as 'pressure of interest', or what Richards[1] describes as 'the state of vigilance' which the reader brings to what is read.

The reader's motivation for reading will have considerable effect upon the character and intensity of his interest. Motivation may be seen to be purposive or diversionary in character. The purposive motivation may be specific or general. The specific is stimulated by some particular need of the reader, as for example the obligation to read for a professional examination; the power of his interest in reading derives from his vocational ambition. On the other hand, the general is stimulated by a desire to improve the reader's cultural level and his personal development; the power of his interest derives from a high degree of mental health—that state of mind which is ever open to intensify its awareness and understanding of reality.

Whereas the purposive motivation may be said to be instrumental, in that it is prompted by the reader's conscious need for economic and personal development, the diversionary motivation is prompted by the need for the reader to change from one activity to another. There is a tendency to view this whole range of reading as 'escapist' in a somewhat derogatory sense. But this would be a superficial view. The need of the reader to change from one activity to another can arise from a variety of causes, among which may be distinguished those which can be described as compensatory, remedial, catalytic and narcotic.

Compensatory reading stems from frustrations such as may result from a form of livelihood which severely limits or renders impossible the satisfaction of the individual's interests and creative propensities. Reading, related to a study of some field of interest unconnected with work for a living, may provide compensation and hardly deserves to be described as an escape from reality.

Remedial reading relates to the need for relaxation and the need for the temporary shutting out of cares and problems, leading to a later renewal of energy and ability to cope. Remedial reading may also embrace that reading undertaken, in certain medical and mental conditions, as part of prescribed therapy and referred to as bibliotherapy. Remedial reading may have a catalytic effect when it results in freeing from immediate pre-occupations an active and alert mind while its unconscious counterpart, undisturbed, grapples with real problems. Music and other arts can serve the same purpose. If, as Koestler[2] argues, the mind oscillates between ' self-assertive ' impulses and ' self-transcending ' or integrating impulses, reading for relaxation may have a deeper personal and social significance than is generally allowed. In normal day-to-day activity the mind tends to be dominated by ' self-assertive ' impulses, whereas, in listening to music or in reading, the mind's impulses are of the integrating order which deepens the awareness of the ' togetherness ' of life. The integrating impulses meet the deep need for the feeling that one is part of the whole.

Reading which may be described as narcotic is perhaps the only truly ' escapist ' reading, in the normally accepted sense that it is motivated by the desire to shut out the impact of external reality when the latter presents apparently insoluble or unwanted problems. Narcotic reading may also occur as a form of pseudo-activity, when reading becomes so much a habit as, say, smoking, that opportunities for reading are seized upon in preference to any other activity. It is the habitual use of reading prompted by these motives which justifies its description as narcotic when otherwise it might more properly be regarded as remedial.

C S Lewis,[3] discussing the subject of types of readers, makes a distinction between ' use ' of art and the appreciation of art; it is the latter which underlies a motivation for reading which is neither especially purposive nor diversionary in character. In this kind of reading the reader appreciates the imaginative powers and insights of the writer and the artistry with which he uses language to express them, and is rewarded with that elusive exhilaration evoked in the expression ' joie de vivre '. Such reading is not sought for its practical possibilities nor, principally, for the insights it may afford, but rather for the delight it offers and the appreciation it evokes; it may appropriately be referred to as appreciative reading.

It is apparent that the reader's comprehension is of a complex nature conditioned by the technical ability to read, mental background and the interest or vigilance brought to reading. Instrumental, compensatory and appreciative reading are associated with a greater intensity of interest brought to reading than is likely to be the case with remedial and narcotic reading, and will correspondingly affect the ' drive ' to comprehension. Interest can be so strong a factor in comprehension that, given some ability to read, it may overcome deficiencies in reading ability and mental background. It must not be overlooked that in the actual process of reading, the possibility exists for the intensity and direction of interest to change, so that what may have originated as a diversionary approach to reading may lead to one of a more purposive character.

There is a variety of cultural and environmental factors which affect the motivations and intensities of interest in reading. There is, for example, a definite correlation between interest in reading and the educational and social level of the reader. Not only does the higher educational level affect the technical ability to read, but it is frequently accompanied by a corresponding level of mental health and attitude. Similarly, the better social and occupational levels of the reader tend to result in a greater propensity for reading. This may be because reading at these levels is more of a traditional activity and they are likely to offer a wider experience of life than at lower levels. Age and increased responsibilities tend to reduce opportunity and interest in reading. It should be of particular significance too to note that potential interest in reading is greater in the adolescent group than in older groups. The availability of time for reading and the degrees of accessibility to appropriate reading materials not only comprise opportunity for reading, but can, at particular times, considerably modify the motivations and interests predominant in the choice of reading.

Readers will tend to fall into groups in which one or the other of the motivations and interests will predominate. Nevertheless, individual readers will pass from one group to another from time to time, will be motivated in varying degrees at different times, and will frequently be affected by a number of motivations simultaneously.

It is not always appreciated that one reader may be inspired by all the varieties of motivation, by one at one time, by a different one at another time, or by a mixture of motivations at one and the same time. Thus there is a tendency to classify readers rather than reading, so that readers are regarded as falling into such exclusive categories as ' purposive ' on the one hand, and ' escapist ' or ' non-purposive ' on the other. Reflection will confirm that our own motives have varied from time to time, and who has not had the experience of visiting a library merely to find something to read (remedial or escapist motivation) and then, by chance, happening upon a book which has stimulated a stronger motivation (either specific or general, but purposive)?

If readers are categorised into distinct groups, then the organisation and arrangement of the library will follow a similar pattern. In fact, libraries do tend to be organised around the ' purposive ' readers; classification is designed with this type of reading in mind and so is shelf arrangement; so much so, that the purposive organisation becomes a barrier, a frustration for the ' non-purposive ' reader. It is sometimes argued that the library should not be concerned with the ' non-purposive ' reader, and if readers could be neatly categorised in this way, perhaps little harm would be done. The effect of so categorising readers is that the reader who at one time is ' purposive ', at another time ' non-purposive ', is, in the latter mood, frustrated by the ' purposive ' arrangement of the library and is frequently lost. For, while the ' purposive ' mood is more intense and specific, it occurs with most of us less frequently than the more generalised ' non-purposive '.

The categorisation of reading rather than readers would suggest a different organisation and arrangement. The reader-oriented library would take into account the complex range of motivations for reading, and the associated differences in pressures of interest which they evoke. Its essential feature must be an arrangement allowing a natural and unimpeded movement of the reader from the conditions appropriate to the ' diversionary ' interests through to those most appropriate to the more ' purposive ' and thus the more intensely specific. Such an arrangement could be described as ' Service in depth '. Figure 2 illustrates the principle applied to a medium sized library. Reception and loan control activities will be located in the entrance foyer, and in any case outside the public stack room. The area nearest the entrance of the room is set out much as an attractive bookshop would be, and

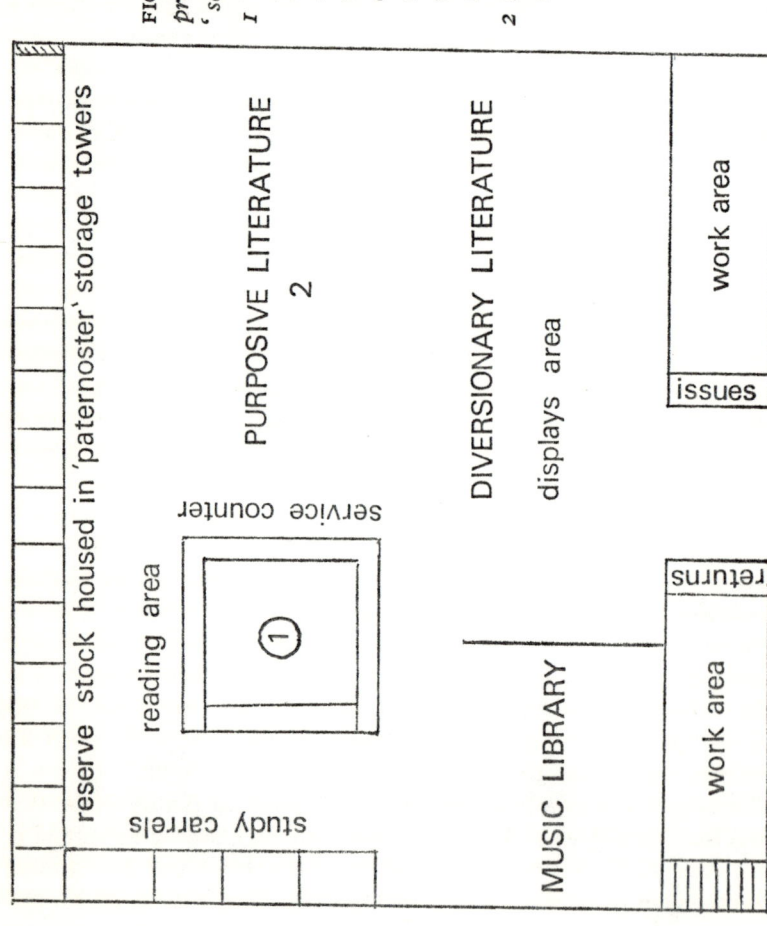

FIGURE 2 *Schematic diagram (non-proportional and not to scale) of 'service in depth' arrangement.*

1 *The central staircase leads up from the service counter to the Bibliographical Department, which is arranged under subject divisions—cataloguing, classification, stock revision, suggestions, requests. Alternative access is by staircase at bottom left.*

2 *Reference and loan material is shelved in a single sequence.*

reserve stock housed in 'paternoster' storage towers

PURPOSIVE LITERATURE
2

DIVERSIONARY LITERATURE

displays area

reading area

service counter

MUSIC LIBRARY

study carrels

work area

issues

returns

work area

houses popular fiction classes and a number of constantly changing book displays likely to be of interest to the 'non-purposive' reader. Beyond this area books are arranged by subjects and include current and classic literature in the best possible condition, reference and loan copies of books being integrated into one sequence. Books not available for loan will be suitably marked. At the rear of the room will be provision for quiet reading areas and study carrels, and access to collections containing books withdrawn from active circulation but still considered to be of value. Periodicals are grouped with appropriate subjects.

Accessibility to the bookstocks has so important a bearing on the reader's choice that although it is neither possible nor entirely desirable for reserve collections to be merged with the current active stock, their availability and ease of access to them deserve special consideration. Ideally, the reader should have ready access to the reserve stack and, preferably, from within the room in which he is studying or working and where books on the open shelves too are at hand. Such an arrangement might be achieved by a stack based on the paternoster lift principle indicated on the plan in figure 2 and whose method of operation is illustrated in figure 3. The lift consists of an endless chain, or two chains in parallel, passing over geared wheels erected vertically to any convenient height. The chains are moved by a power unit which can be stopped at any position required. Freely suspended between the chains are book trays or shelves so that they retain a vertical position when moving round top or bottom of the lift. Thus a lift could be mounted to a height of say thirty feet, allowing room for up to sixty shelves. A series of such lifts could be erected side by side enclosed within an insulated prefabricated shell with openings provided at the reader level. The openings would be protected by glass sliding doors which could be controlled to open only when the lift is stopped in the required position. The openings would be large enough to enable a reader to examine up to 150 books at a glance. The lift would be controlled by the user so that by an indexed series of buttons or switches he could bring into access any portion of the stack desired. Apart from the advantages to the reader, problems related to economy of space, heating, lighting and fire precaution would be minimised.

Between the 'diversionary' and 'purposive' areas of the room is set the service counter as the spearhead of the bibliographical and professional services. This is the heart of the library; behind or above the service counter, but with access to it, the whole of the professional

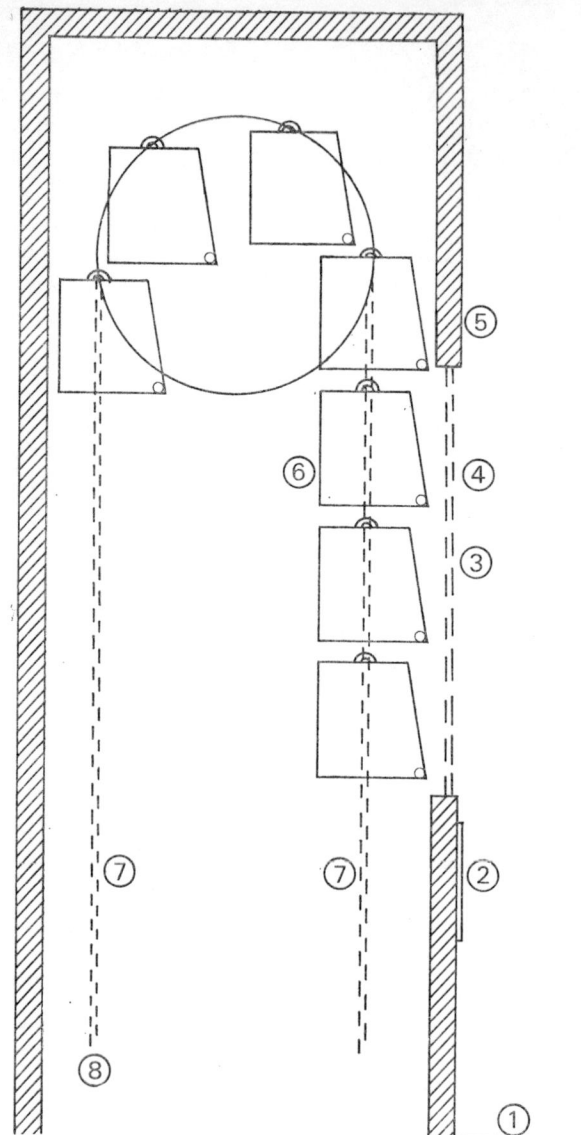

FIGURE 3   *Paternoster Book Store.*

Top floor of a series of levels as capacity demands. 1 foot height of tower will provide capacity for 100 volumes, eg 30' tower will house 3,000 volumes. 10 tower floors will house 30,000 volumes.

1 *Floor level;* 2 *Control panel to bring any one block of shelves to door position as required;* 3 *Reader access to give visibility to approximately 150 volumes;* 4 *Sliding doors openable only when wheel is static;* 5 *Rubber roller to edge of shelf;* 6 *Flexible shelf unit 6' wide with centre partition to give* 2 × 3' *shelves;* 7 *Flexible chains connected by rods from which are hung free swinging shelves;* 8 *To lower levels.*

ability of the staff can be brought to bear on service to the reader. The staff at this point would have available the best collection of bibliographical tools that the library could afford, together with the master catalogue of all books in stock throughout the system and currently on order from suppliers or other sources, and would have direct access to all the main book collections including files and reserve stocks.

Such an arrangement would call for a particular organisation of staff. So far as practicable, all administrative and clerical work would be separated out from professional duties and performed by administrative and clerical workers. The processes of classification, cataloguing, stock maintenance, all bibliographical work and work with readers would be grouped under a distinct section emerging at the main service point for work with readers. Only experienced and trained professional staff would make contact with readers, while the junior assistants would assist in the various tasks of the section. The bringing together of professional lending, reference and technical staffs would permit the organisation of the section to be based on subject specialisation. Broad sections of the stock would become the responsibility of sub-divisions of the staff under a subject librarian. The duties of each sub-division would include : stock development and maintenance, classification, cataloguing, bibliographical work and assistance to readers within the area of subject specialisation. The work of the various sub-divisions would be under the supervision of a co-ordinating officer-in-charge of the whole section.

A reader-orientated arrangement on the lines suggested would reduce the risk of frustration for the reader whatever the type of interest predominant at any one time; as his interest became more purposive and thus more intense, the incentive to move towards more specialised facilities would arise naturally. The staff would be organised towards the central objective of service to readers, and the advantages of a measure of subject specialisation would be possible. Both physical arrangement and service would be organised in depth.

REFERENCES

1 Richards, I A : *Practical criticism.* Kegan Paul, 1949.
2 Koestler, Arthur : *Insight and outlook.* Macmillan, 1949.
3 Lewis, C S : *An experiment in criticism.* CUP, 1961.

4: *New concepts of service*

THE public library service, because it is a social institution, and because its services are freely available to all, must benefit society as a whole. As society is composed of individuals, it follows that the non-user must benefit as well as the user. The service does not exist simply to meet a *demand* for books. Although the satisfaction of individual demands for books may be the way in which the purposes are achieved, it is because the reading of books and the freely available opportunity for reading them are believed to result in values for all that the public library service is financed from public funds. If the same results could be more economically obtained by a system for the free distribution of cabbages, the existence of a demand for books would not necessarily lead to the setting up of a public library system.

The availability of books and the reading of them appear to produce results not achieved, or not so well achieved, in other ways. These results seem to me to derive, firstly, from the individual's reading, and, secondly, from the nature of the public library system and its part in the social structure.

In the process of reading books, the reader may gain awareness. By this I mean knowledge and experience. He may increase perception, by which I mean an understanding of relationships existing in life and among people. He may also exercise imagination, by which I mean the faculty of insight and the ability to project himself into the life of others. The enrichment and development of the individual, thus possible, is not only of value in itself, but is clearly valuable to society. There are other more directly social consequences. For example, in the complex urban society of today, the reading of books reduces tension for the individual and thus contributes to the mental health and stability of society. Almost as a by-product of his reading, the reader is prepared for the accepted patterns of conduct among the various groups in society, to which at one time or another the individual must become attached, and in which he has to play his part. These and other benefits which the individual may gain from the reading of books are available from agencies other than the public library. The particular contribution

44

made by the public library here is the guarantee which it offers that all, without let or hindrance, can participate, and that the opportunity for the maximum social benefit exists.

But there are other consequences which appear to me to be of particular importance in modern society. These derive solely from the existence of the public library as a universal institution. The public library is the only channel of communication of ideas and feelings which is not now controlled either by powerful minority interests or by monopolies. The public library uniquely affords the expression of all minority views, gives all of them the opportunity of acceptance, or of withering away. Its existence in the form we know is a guarantee of intellectual and political freedom. It is essential to the development and flow of ideas, and to the increase of perception. But the public library, by its provision for the widest range of minority expression, serves also another valuable social purpose. The individual cannot exist in isolation. He belongs to various groups—the family, the factory, the nation, and many more besides. The price of his acceptance into the group is conformity to the group's requirements of conduct. As an individual he is unique, so that no group completely satisfies his need for expression. He is always at variance, in greater or lesser degree, with his group. He needs strongly, however, to feel confirmed in those feelings and ideas where he is at variance. If he cannot avoid feeling ' alone ' he will be tempted to compel others to agree with him or to indulge in anti-social activity. Because the economics of book production enable even the most subtle variations in ideas and feelings to be published, and the public library makes widespread distribution possible, the individual, through reading, is able to seek out ideas and feelings similar to those of his own. Thus the more effective the public library system, and the more sensitive it is to the provision of minority expression, the more readily will individuals avoid frustration.

If these seem to be very high purposes, perhaps too broad or even vague for practical use, I can only say that I find it necessary to come back to them constantly when assessing the organisation of a service, or when in need of assurance as to the validity of what I am doing. They confirm for me overriding considerations. We provide books not merely because some people want them; we provide books because their widest dissemination is a social necessity. The most effective group of readers to aim at in planning is that comprising readers between, say, 15 and 35 years of age. It is this group from which the maximum benefits can be derived. For it is during this period that the individual is most

45

open to extend his knowledge and to increase his perception. The proportion of people who have passed through the public library service is, I think, more useful in assessing its value than the proportion of the total population who may, at any given time, be members.

Whatever purposes we may consider the public library exists to serve, it can hardly be denied that it is through the provision of books that we have to achieve them. Our main problem, then, is concerned with the provision of books.

I should explain, of course, that by the term 'Provision of books' I mean the provision of books to be read. So the problem of book provision is concerned very much with the readers as well as with books. In fact, I would say that successful book provision results from the integration of three broad factors in individual reader transactions.

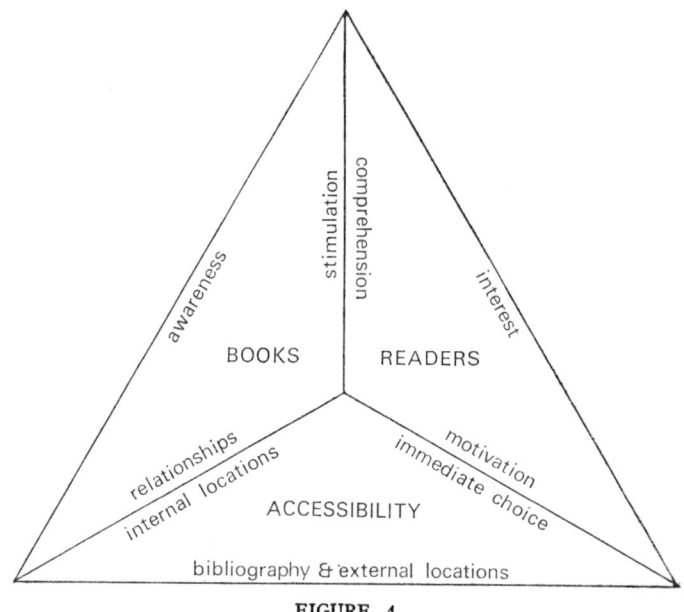

FIGURE 4

I like to visualise the problem in the form of a diagram (figure 4) which comprises a large triangle of three equal sides. This triangle represents successful book provision, and it is sub-divided into three smaller and equal triangles, each representing an essential factor. The three inner triangles represent respectively, readers, books and accessibility. Unless all three are present and adequately taken into account,

46

the large triangle, representing successful book provision, cannot be completed. The sides of the smaller triangles represent characteristics which must be encompassed when assessing the effects or requirements of the three components of book provision. Differences in any characteristics will, naturally, affect the total result. If we take the three inner triangles separately, the triangle representing *readers* has three sides designated respectively interest, comprehension, motivation, the triangle representing *books* has three sides designated respectively awareness, relationships, stimulation; and the triangle representing *accessibility* has three sides designated respectively immediate choice, internal locations, bibliography and external locations.

The attitude and approach of the reader modifies the outcome of his reading. The aspects of the reader noted in the triangle designated *readers* are those which need to be taken into account.

Comprehension—denotes the level of experience and the technical ability to read. The level of comprehension must be taken into account.

Interest—denotes subject interest of reader. This aspect is of most importance in determining what kinds of books are to be provided.

Motivation—denotes what stimulates the reader's interest, for upon the motive to reading depends the strength or power of his interest. This aspect has bearing on the arrangement of books in the library, and the nature of the service provided. I think we may distinguish two broad motivations: relaxing, which may be either escapist or genuinely relaxing; purposive, which may be either general or specific. Specific interest is the strongest and escapist interest is the weakest. I have elaborated these ideas in previous papers.[1]

The value of books for our purpose lies in their effects on readers. So that, in considering the *books* to be provided, we need to look for qualities which support the purposes of the public library system and which I have earlier put forward:

Awareness—denotes factual knowledge, exposition of what is, has been or will be.

Relationship—denotes the how and why principle, the exposition of skills, mental and manual, relationships.

Stimulation—denotes the emotional effects of the book, the impulse to think, feel and do—it is the creative and imaginative aspect. It includes empathy or identification with others.

The extent, authority and skill with which one or more of these aspects are presented in the book determines its value or quality for book provision. But even if eligible on this score it must be related to the subject interest of the reader and the level of his comprehension.

If book provision is to be effective, the right book and the right reader must be brought together at the right time. The third major factor, therefore is *accessibility*. The three aspects noted in the accesibility triangle denote degrees of accessibility available to the reader at any particular time and are:

Immediate choice—denoting book required is on the shelves when the reader requires it.

Internal locations—denotes not immediately available, being either on loan to another reader or located elsewhere in the library system, *eg* at branch library, in binding, withdrawals pending, reserve stock, etc.

Bibliography and external locations—denotes use of bibliographies to indicate existence of right book leading to external locations, *ie* sources for books outside the library system, *eg* inter-lending schemes, book trade, legal and medical subscription libraries, etc.

Accessibility is the achilles heel of the public library system. Getting the book to the reader at the time he wants it is the greatest practical difficulty with which we are faced and is one to which we have given insufficient attention, particularly in the internal organisation of the library system. The importance of this factor has been evident in the steady growth and improvement of inter-lending schemes in recent years.

The growth of co-operation and inter-lending also points to a considerable change in our conception of the proper limits of book provision, and which the schema I have outlined fully supports. Our main professional task should no longer be described as book selection, but book provision. If the reader is to get the right book, the whole field of literature in his subject field must be accessible to him. This calls for emphasis on bibliographical knowledge as the prime qualification of the librarian, and organisation designed to give the maximum degree of accessibility for the reader.

If book provision is the main problem, the analysis of the factors involved not only facilitates the actual task of provision, but offers guidance as to the forms of organisation needed to make it effective.

The way in which we see the problem of book provision obviously affects the organisation of staff, the arrangement of books and the various practical methods employed. The knowledge of books is so important a requirement in each factor of book provision that an organisation of staff based on bibliography seems self-evident. I have described such an arrangement of staff in my paper ' The organisation of a public library for subject specialisation '.[2] I venture to deal with this here, therefore, in outline only.

The techniques and processes of librarianship are subordinated to the main bibliographical function. Professional staff are sub-divided into subject groups, each of which is responsible for a subject field of the book stock throughout the system. The subject group's duties include acquisition and revision of the book stock, classification and cataloguing, readers' inquiries and requests, and bibliography within the subject field. The work of all the groups is co-ordinated by a senior officer. As it is necessary for the professional staff to be in continuous contact with readers, all serve on a rota for readers advisory duty at all libraries. The effect of the arrangement is that professional staff are handling books and readers at all stages continuously. The knowledge of readers is not divorced from the knowledge of books.

In order that the time of the professional staff is used to the maximum on professional tasks, a parallel division of staff deals with all administrative, clerical and general duties. Wherever possible, routine and clerical operations are separated out from professional duties and are performed by appropriate staff. This permits a higher degree of centralisation of routine work and further economises in the use of staff.

The division of work into professional and non-professional is not absolutely essential to a bibliographical organisation of staff. It does, however, follow very naturally from it, and I am certain that it makes possible a fuller use of the professional staff.

The kind and level of interest of the reader has such a considerable effect on his approach to reading that it must underlie the arrangement of book stock within a library and as between libraries. The arrangement should be designed to facilitate the movement of the reader in accordance with his level of interest, ensuring that, as his interest becomes more specific or purposive, the incentive to move towards more specialised facilities arises naturally. I have coined the phrase ' service in depth ' to describe this principle, and it is more fully elaborated in earlier papers and articles.[3, 2] The main features of the arrangement are the shelving of books in the main library room so that the more popular and current literature is the first to be met by readers, with advanced and reference material and specialised collections readily accessible from the same public area, but necessarily at a more distant position. At a position roughly midway between the two main levels of book stock is placed the information service counter, the staff of which should have ready access to all collections, including the reserve stack. The charging and discharging processes take place outside the main public room. Once in the main library the readers can only turn for assistance to the professionally trained staff. Experience with two libraries arranged on this plan shows that a marked increase takes place both in the number and level of inquiries from readers. Correspondingly, a higher level of service is demanded. The same principle operates between libraries within a system and between the system as a whole and other systems. As a general rule it is possible to locate advanced and specialised literature in the central library, where the reader's interest is strong enough to accept a lower degree of accessibility. Similarly, when borrowing from other libraries, requests can be limited to advanced and specialised material for which the system's own readership is too small to warrant purchase.

The combination of staff organisation and library arrangement which I have outlined does integrate bibliographical practice with knowledge of readers' requirements *at the point of service*. Thus the triangles of book provision are expressed in a practical unity.

This paper has necessarily been confined to concepts rather than practical methods. But it will be clear that the kind of organisation which follows from them will involve reconsideration of many of the methods employed in the conventional public library system. As book provision is our main task, the methods employed in connection with it have, naturally, changed considerably. Some account of the methods developed may, therefore, be of interest, and will also serve to show how the basic concepts have been interpreted in method.

Each subject group is allocated a budget for book purchase and is responsible for purchases, revision of stock, readers' requests and reservation and rebinding within its subject field. In each subject group one assistant librarian has special responsibility for supervision of the book stock in one library, and the appropriate assistant librarians are consulted with regard to allocation of copies. The subject groups have considerable discretion in the day-to-day purchase of books, but apart from current material they are expected to build up desiderata lists for the revision of their book stocks, and which they discuss with me before final decisions as to purchase are made. When allocating the book fund initially, I hold in reserve under my personal control about 10 percent of it which I use to deal with heavy special requirements, or to adjust the subject group budgets from time to time during the year should that prove necessary. In the matter of purchases to satisfy requests or reservations, it is only necessary to refer to me if a decision has been made neither to purchase nor to borrow.

In preparing desiderata a simple card is used (it is also used as a manuscript catalogue card). It gives the usual description of the book suggested, but in addition allows for an indication of copies already in stock, the level of interest which the book may be expected to satisfy and a series of stock control figures. These stock control figures are extracted from the stock control record which shows, for the subject in which the book falls, what kind of stock action is called for in the next twelve months, and what action has taken place to date.

		Year	April	May
a	Number in issue			
b	Number on shelves			
c	Total a & b			
d	$a \times$			
e	$d \times 2$			
f	$e - c$			
g	$f \div$			
h	$g \times$			
	Total withdrawals to date			
	Proportion year's additions to date			
	Total additions to date			
	Cost to date			
	SUBJECT No			

FIGURE 5: STOCK CONTROL RECORD

against (d) is placed no of books per reader factor.

against (g) is placed depreciation period.

against (h) is placed average cost per volume in previous year.

The stock control record, as its name implies, is the means by which overall control of the state of the book stock in all subjects, as disposed in all the libraries, is maintained.

A description of the basic entry comprising the stock control record will help to make its uses clearer. A record card is kept for each of about 150 subject divisions of the book stock and separately for each library in the system. Under monthly headings are entered the number of books in the issue trays on a fixed day in each month, and the number of books found to be on the shelves on that same day. This 'count' as we refer to it, is done on the last Wednesday of each month. Detailed records of issue figures are no longer kept. The two figures thus produced on the card are combined to show the number of books in circulation at the time of the count. You will note that this figure takes care of all movements of stock into and out of circulation. Thus there is no need to record the number of books at binding or returned from binding and so on. The count simply shows the number of books available on that day. Additional provision under monthly heads is made for total withdrawals to-date, total additions to date and the total cost of the additions to date. Immediately below the 'count' figures are spaces which permit a short series of simple calculations to be made and which produce the results of a formula to which I will refer later. The object of the calculations is to produce a figure which can serve as a rough guide to the number of books required in the subject so that the stock can be completely replaced in a given depreciation period. The depreciation period varies with the subjects, and is fixed to ensure that no book remains in stock which is out of date or in poor condition. Those falling under the broad heading of science and technology work to a period of 10 years, subjects within the humanities work to a period of 15 years. In the case of fiction, light-fiction works to a period based on actual withdrawals due to poor physical condition, and all other fiction works to a period of not more than five years. These depreciation periods are of particular use when we are concerned with the revision of stock.

In day-to-day references by the subject librarians these cards offer readily visible information which can be valuable to them in a number of ways. We assume that the count figure showing the number of books on issue from month to month is sufficiently accurate as an indication of the number of readers continuously reading in the subject. Thus the subject librarian knows the number of readers in the subject, and this can help him when assessing the proportions of different levels of interest to cater for. For example, a subject having a continuous readership of over 100 is likely to be able to accept a number of books at quite advanced level, whereas a subject with a continuous readership of, say, 5 would have to be considered very much more carefully in this respect. It would also make a difference according to whether the cards related to branches or to the central library. The immediate comparison possible between the number of readers and the number of books continuously left on the shelves is also significant. For example, a subject showing, say, 5 percent only of its stock continuously on the shelves would suggest without doubt the need for more books, whereas if the position were reversed and the subject showed 95 percent of its stock continuously on the shelves, some urgent investigation of the condition of that book stock would be called for. In practice, the continual use of these records gives much finer indications than the extremes I have quoted. By keeping the cards for the separate libraries together under the one subject heading, comparisons between libraries are easy to make, and assist in decisions to allocate copies as between libraries. The relative urgency of revision and investigation of stock are also thereby indicated. By the inclusion of figures showing withdrawals and additions to date the subject librarian can readily see (as the year progresses), the results of his own actions on the book stock.

I think the particular value of this kind of stock control record lies in its indication of the number of books which are continuously left on the shelves. For the great majority of the readers their immediate choice is confined to those books which happen to be on the shelves when they use the library. No matter how good the stock which is out, and if it is good stock it is likely to be out most of the time, the reader's choice is limited to what is in. The ratio between the books *in* and the books *out* shown on the record has proved to be very accurate as a guide to the state of the book stocks in all subjects. These figures, therefore, are used to assess the need for stock revision, which is treated as a continuous process. By using the kardex type of visible record it is possible to use the visible edges of the cards to take removable signals. To give the subject librarians a programme and guide to stock revision for twelve months ahead, I simply examine all the cards, and in accordance with the indications given by the records I insert signals showing either that a subject needs revision or needs additional stock, or even both. By the use of more than one signal I can also indicate the degree of priority of attention called for in each case. Whatever defects this type of record may have in other respects, it is uncannily accurate in showing the sections of stock which need investigation or attention. It has also the great advantage that the need for revision in any one subject is not overlooked, as it may be if revision depends solely on personal inspection. The only reservation I would make about its use is that it must not be interpreted too literally. It is primarily an indicator of trends rather than of fixed quantities. It is a tool requiring the application of judgement.

The actual method of revision of stock is simple. Where the signals on the stock control record indicate need for revision, the subject group notes the period of depreciation shown on the card. All books published before this depreciation figure (in the case of non-fiction, 10 or 15 years), are removed from the shelves. Subject to reasonable physical condition, books showing issues in the last two years and books of standard value (but only after my inspection or the inspection of the senior librarian-in-charge of subject groups) are returned to the shelves. Any other books which the subject librarian considers should be returned to circulation are set aside for inspection and approval. Books which it is agreed should be returned to the shelves, but which are in poor physical condition or are unattractive in appearance, are withdrawn and a desiderata card for replacement is made out. From the balance of withdrawn books those which are last copies in the region, or are advanced or specialised works still of some current value, are transferred to reserve stock. The remaining books are permanently withdrawn. Following the completion of the withdrawal process, desiderata lists for improvement of the section are prepared, if this is considered necessary, by the subject librarian. If the revision has not been adequate —this will quickly show itself on the stock control record and it will be signalled for further attention.

The stock control record has a further important use—that is, in the calculation of the book budgets for the subject librarians and the total annual book fund requirement. Over a period a formula has been evolved for these purposes. It contains one 'rule of thumb' factor which I am still experimenting with and which I hope ultimately, will be determined more positively. The items used in the formula are as follows : —

$a=$the number of readers in the subject field (this is taken off the stock control record—the count figure showing the highest number of books on issue in any one month is used).

$b=$volumes per reader required to ensure adequate selection for all levels of reading (assuming broad levels of popular, intermediate and advanced) in the subject. This factor is determined experimentally and is the one which in some cases is still arbitrary. At present the factors used are:

central library   fiction 1.5   non-fiction 8.0
branch libraries   fiction 2.0   non-fiction 6.0.

The differences as between central and branch libraries are designed to allow for a higher proportion of books at an advanced level to be allocated to the central library.

c=number of volumes at present in circulation in the subject field. (This is obtained by adding together the count figures for books on issue and books on shelves.)

d=period of depreciation. (This also is taken off the stock control record and varies between subjects as follows:

Non-fiction—science & technology	10 years
Non-fiction—humanities	15 years
Fiction (other than light fiction)	5 years
Light fiction—the percent of withdrawals to stock in the year.	

e=average cost per volume in previous year (also taken from stock control record).

The formula itself is:

$$\left\{ \frac{2(a \times b) - c}{d} \right\} \times e$$

By a particular arrangement of the entries on the stock control record the result of this formula for each subject is arrived at by a series of short and simple calculations. To find the book fund budget for a subject librarian, it is necessary only to add up the results for each of the subjects falling to this group. The total of all the cards produces the total book fund requirement. Should the book fund authorised be less than the book fund required, it is easy to see the effect over the whole of the book stock and to make adjustments accordingly. The operation of the formula varies with and continuously reflects:

the increase or decrease in number of readers actively using the libraries;

variations in depreciation including adequacy or otherwise of the number of books rebound;

variations in cost per volume over all subjects from year to year;

changes in the interests of readers in the various subjects;

variations in all the above as between individual libraries in the system.

It also ensures, if the authorised book fund is equal to the calculated requirement, that the whole of the book stock can be replaced in the periods of depreciation used in the formula.

I have described the stock control system rather fully because it is probably unusual and illustrates better than anything else how the organisation works. (A further development of this system of stock control is described in chapter 8.) But the concepts which I have outlined earlier have involved a continuous revision of all our methods. This has led, in some cases, to simplification and in others to elimination. New methods have also been developed. The problem which I am most concerned with at present is the difficult one of speeding up the processes of getting books to readers. In this connection, I am experimenting with the possibility of some form of movements index which would show with, say, not more than a twenty-four hours time lag, the location of all books temporarily out of circulation. Its object would be to avoid fruitless internal requests between libraries for books which are eventually proved not to be available. If one allows that the degree of accessibility for the readers is an important part in successful book provision, then an efficient means of knowing where books actually are is as important as knowing that the books are in stock.

In conclusion, I deal with a few queries which have been raised from time to time. It has been said that the division of staff into professional and non-professional leads to superfluity of staff. Nothing could be further from the facts. What does happen is that for the first time one begins to appreciate how much work there is in librarianship if the job is to be effectively done. References to practice in the United States are not relevant in this connection—the conditions affecting recruitment and organisation are totally different.

Another question which has been raised is to what extent the scheme I have described is exportable to other library systems. In larger systems I can see no difficulty at all. The number of subject groups could be increased slightly, but if the number of libraries in the system is greater than the number of desirable subject groups, it should be possible to base the groups on the equivalent of district libraries. In very small systems, of course, some degree of co-operation with other neighbouring systems would be essential, and to be effective nothing short of an actual merger would do. It does seem that to obtain the full advantages of professional skill and service a minimum size of authority is necessary. However, I think that once the basic principles are accepted, then implementation in a greater or lesser degree is possible in most libraries.

It would be wrong to imply from what I have said that any sort of ideal system has been devised. What I have tried to do is to develop a system based on a consistent set of concepts about the purposes of a public library. Emphasis has been placed on the bibliographical function of the librarian and the need for continuous relationship with the readers.

REFERENCES

1 McClellan, A W: 'Reading as communication'. *Library world,* October 1949. (See chapter 3.)

2 McClellan, A W: 'The organisation of a public library for subject specialisation'. *Library Association record,* August 1955. (See chapter 5.)

3 McClellan, A W: 'Service in depth'. *Library world,* April 1950. (See chapter 3.)

5: The organisation of a library for subject specialisation

THE idea of subject specialisation in the organisation of public libraries is not new. The arrangement of libraries into subject departments has been commonly practised in the United States, and even in this country more limited attempts have been made. For many years Dr Savage propounded the idea. I think there may be at least two reasons why it has not taken in this country.

As practised, both in the United States and in this country, it has taken the form of setting up distinct departments which become in effect separate libraries within a library. The scale of resources required to contemplate such an arrangement has been sufficient to deter any but the largest library systems. Another weakness of the arrangement is the underlying assumption that readers fall into distinct categories, whereas in fact the individual general reader, for whom our public libraries largely cater, is potentially interested in a variety of fields of literature. Consequently, physically distinct subject departments could well have an inhibiting effect so far as the majority of our readers are concerned. The traditional separation of our reference libraries gives evidence of this effect. When a high standard of assistance to readers is available in lending libraries, the number of typically reference inquiries received in them is high and the readers making these inquiries would not in many cases have considered the possibility of using the reference library.

The combination of the removal of the penny rate limitation and the widespread adoption of the open-access system about the period of 1920 was responsible for an extensive development in public library organisation. This development proceeded on lines which were not conducive to the idea of subject specialisation. I believe that the particular type of organisation which developed from about 1920 accounts for the fact, more than does anything else, that subject specialisation did not become the basic principle of organisation in our public libraries.

Prior to 1920 the typical library unit was small in scale. The chief librarian was frequently the only experienced professional officer and he did almost everything required to run his library. He was both bookman and administrator, he knew most of his readers personally, he selected, purchased, edited, classified and catalogued his bookstock. Rather belatedly, perhaps, we now acknowledge what excellent basic bookstocks were built up by these predecessors of ours. The extent of administration was small and the chief was primarily a bookman who knew his books and his readers intimately.

With the removal of the penny rate limitation and the introduction of the open-access system there occurred also a rapid expansion in the demands on public library services. There followed a tremendous increase in service points, books and readers. The typical library system became a much larger organisation with larger staffs. Some division of labour or a degree of specialisation became essential.

What form did this division of labour take? The organisation of the library was adapted to the immediate and obvious needs. The immediate problems were concerned with the handling of large quantities of books and the servicing of large numbers of readers. In the one case the obvious solution was to break down the handling of books into the various book processes, selection, purchase, classification, cataloguing, etc; in the other, the extension of accommodation and service points. Later the advantages of centralising these processes in the hands of specialists divorced from the service points became widely accepted. The year 1939 probably saw the closing phase of the extension of physical units of service, and the post war years have witnessed the intensification of specialised library techniques.

As the saturation point in the development of these tendencies approached, the tradition of bibliographical assistance to readers reasserted itself. Following naturally what had now become the typical form of specialisation, assistance to readers became a separate specialisation parallel with specialisations in cataloguing and classification. The development of specialist readers advisers stimulated a return to specialisation in bibliography. This was aided by the concurrent growth in the provision of special libraries in industry and elsewhere. In turn a specialisation in stock revision became inevitable and the last in the line of specialists we know as the stock-editor. More recently the idea of a broad division of staffs into professional and non-professional has gained ground.

The typical organisation of a public library currently, therefore, comprises a whole series of specialists, classifiers, cataloguers, readers advisers, stock editors and administrative clerical personnel, plus the sub-stratum of counter and routine assistants in the non-professional category.

Did we take the right turning in the 1920's? With the exception of the specialist readers' adviser, all our experienced professional staffs aim to become specialists cut off from the readers they serve. The great thing is to get away from the public area. Classification and cataloguing take place in a rarified atmosphere uncontaminated by contact with ultimate users or benefactors. How can you catalogue if you never see your catalogues in use, or perhaps do not even know whether your catalogue is used? How select and edit book stocks if seldom meeting those for whom the books are intended?

What do our readers really require of us. I suggest it is a knowledge of books, a knowledge of books related to a knowledge of the readers' needs. Surely this should be our special and characteristic contribution? It is this which should mark us off from other skilled professions. The techniques and processes on which we concentrate are essential tools which are not unique to us, and which should be subordinate to the main bibliographical function.

After 1920, a new division of labour became necessary, but it might have been better to have been based on bibliography, rather than on techniques and methods.

' The right book (or the right piece of information), to the right reader at the right time.' This hackneyed phrase still epitomises our purpose better perhaps, than any other. If fully effective it could revolutionise the meaning of public library service. It is useful to note that the phrase falls into three parts—knowledge of books and sources, knowledge of readers, and administrative efficiency in marrying the two. The object of our organisation must be to integrate these three *at the point of service*. We need, therefore, an organisation of resources (books, staff and buildings) which will serve primarily bibliographical activities which are intimately linked with the readers for whom the activities exist.

Except in the smallest public library, it is no longer possible for one professional officer to cope with all the bibliographical requirements of a service. Merely to add portions of bibliographical work to the duties of technical and process specialists will result in the techniques and processes receiving the greater priority because these are the special responsibilities of the staffs concerned. Another weakness of this arrangement lies in the fact that these technical specialists are increasingly divorced from day-to-day contact with readers and it is essential that bibliographical work should be constantly related to the readers.

If bibliographical activity is to be the dominant theme in the pattern of organisation, any sub-division of work will have to follow bibliographical lines. The first unit of sub-division therefore, becomes a subject field within the whole field of knowledge.

The organisation of a library service on this principle cuts right across the customary arrangement—it is not easy to abandon habits of mind long acquired and quite new practical problems present themselves. The description of an ideal organisation based on subject-specialisation is less interesting and useful than to submit an outline of a practical attempt to carry it out. Despite the fact that we have certainly not solved all the problems involved, I propose to tell you how we have tried to deal with subject-specialisation in my own system. The practical application of a general conception of this kind affects the definition and distribution of duties, the physical arrangement of books and buildings and the administration and control of the organisation. I will describe our experiments, therefore, under these heads.

The principal activities of the system are covered by two broad divisions of staff, namely, the Administrative and General Duties Division and the Bibliographical Division. In addition there are divisions responsible for special collections (which includes the Local History Department) and for work with young people. These two divisions can be ignored for the purpose of illustrating the theme of this paper.

The Administration Division consists of a number of groups: the General Administration Group—comprising general administration, establishment work, accounts, statistics and returns, registration, etc; A Typing Group; a Technical Services Group including printing and binding, artists and photographer; a Public Service and General Duties Group which includes a central pool of trainees and general duties assistants. Excluding specialist and technical staffs this division has an allocation of staff of one chief administrative assistant, one administrative assistant, three clerical assistants, two shorthand/typists, twenty-seven general assistants and up to six library trainees.

The Bibliographical Division consists of five subject groups, each responsible for a broad subject division of the bookstocks throughout the system, including the appropriate reference stocks. In addition, each group has a special responsibility for one library in the system. The division has an allocation of staff of one senior librarian-in-charge (who acts as coordinating officer), four librarians-in-charge and ten assistant librarians. Each group takes a staff of one librarian-in-charge and two assistant librarians. One assistant librarian in each group is assigned specific responsibility for one of the five libraries.

Each subject group within the *subject field allocated to it* has the following specific duties: Prepare desiderata lists for my consideration, select and purchase books within broad terms of reference, allocate books between libraries; classify and catalogue all books and material; revision of stock; screening of withdrawn books; screening of books for rebinding; maintenance of central reserve stocks; bibliographical work including compilation of special lists and indexes; the bibliographical aspects of inter-library and regional loans and of readers' requests and reservations; readers' advisory and information service.

The senior librarian-in-charge in the division coordinates the work of the subject librarians. For example, he settles problems concerning book purchases in marginal subjects when these cannot be settled between the subject librarians involved. Each group is responsible for the activities mentioned, over the whole system. Readers' inquiries which cannot be dealt with when they originate are passed to the appropriate subject group for attention. These are frequently answered by post.

All the assistants in this division cover the readers' advisory service by regular periods of duty in the various libraries. To preserve continuity, of course, the same assistants cover between them the same library. This arrangement also enables each group to maintain a general oversight of one particular library.

The effects of this arrangement can be seen in two ways. The subject group librarian is concerned all the time with books and inquiries about books. From his book selection and stock revision work he is familiar with book sources. He is in contact with regional sources and appropriate special libraries. He handles all the books that come into or go out of circulation. Through his readers' information work he is in continuous contact with his readers. Above all he is constantly improving his practical knowledge of bibliography. All the important techniques in which he has been trained are in continuous use. No aspect of his ability as a professional librarian is allowed to run to seed through lack of opportunity to use it. Compare his position with that of the librarian of the typical library unit of the pre-1920 period. The valuable characteristics associated with the latter are incorporated in the new arrangement with two qualifications. The burden of administrative routine is almost entirely eliminated, but the field of book provision is more limited.

The reader on the other hand turns for help to the professional staff; he learns to appreciate that his needs are not restricted by the limitations of the bookstock of one library. He learns also to appreciate the possibilities open to him from using the skills of the professional librarian versed in bibliography and at home in the world of books. The arrangement makes possible a more intensive personal service and at the same time stimulates it.

It will be clear already that a very considerable separation of duties requiring professional training and experience, from those of an administrative, clerical or general nature has taken place. We have taken this as far as it is possible to go. Every job has been analysed with a view to removing from the professionally qualified staffs any operation which can be performed by administrative, technical, clerical or unqualified staffs. It is inevitable that this cannot be achieved 100 percent. For example, the subject librarians must write out order cards for the books they decide shall be purchased. The order card having been written out it is passed to the Administration Division which deals with the rest of the procedure up to the marking-off of the book and its delivery to the subject librarian who ordered it.

The relationship between the Bibliographical Division and the Administration Division may be more easily understood if one sees the first as comprising the fighting branch of an army and the second as the supporting services. The Administration Division controls all staffs who are not employed on tasks requiring professional library experience and training, even to branch library level. Each division has its own overall time-sheet. The senior officers of these divisions coordinate all tasks and the time-sheets. Difficulties which they cannot solve are settled by means of a conference under my chairmanship.

The Administration Division controls also a central pool of staff, the members of which are not permanently allocated to any library or work unit. The pool serves to meet shortage of staff at any point in the system, provides staff to clear up arrears of work which may arise from any cause and is available to assist in any special or irregular task. The pool consists of library trainees who are recruited at the end of school terms, in advance of establishment vacancies, and more experienced assistants who are not on professional grades. By service in the pool, trainees gain experience on elementary tasks in all sections of the system, and the more experienced assistants get opportunities for assisting in the work of the Bibliographical Division. The whole arrangement, although ensuring that professionally qualified staffs are fully used for professional work, gives many opportunities for those who are not on professional grades to gain experience in professional tasks. I am at pains to mention this because it is sometimes alleged that the principle of professional and non-professional work denies opportunity to the non-professional. It need not be so at all. There is a difference between dividing tasks into professional and non-professional and dividing staffs into those categories. The first is not too difficult and can be relatively rigid, but the allocation of staffs can be flexible.

The need for the services of the Bibliographical Division to be continuously and obviously available to the readers is an essential part of the subject specialisation arrangement, both in the interest of the readers and of the staffs concerned. It is also necessary that the professional staff on public service duty should have ready access to all the main bookstocks including the major working tool, the bibliographical collection. These requirements call for a particular arrangement of the bookstocks and the public rooms.[1] In the plans for our new central library, which have recently been approved, I have incorporated these ideas.

The charging and discharging processes take place outside the main public room. The first portion of the room consists of an informal reading and smoking lounge in which small book displays can be arranged. There follows an area in which the fiction and popular non-fiction sections are housed on straight-run wall shelving and occasional alcove shelving, together with display bookstands. Informal seating and tables are provided. The bookstocks are grouped under broad interest headings rather than by the straightforward Dewey classification. This part of the room is designed to give the appearance of a large but attractive bookshop. At the far end of the room are the remaining lending and reference books arranged in the same sequence and in the more or less customary class order.

The main feature of the arrangement, however, is the provision, at the junction of the popular section and the general lending and reference collections, of an information service counter. This forms the focal point of the room and from it will operate the subject specialist staffs. The most used reference books are located near the counter and the bibliographical collection will be immediately to hand. The counter will control access to private study carrels which are adjoining. Immediately below the counter, with access by stairs and booklift, is the central reserve stack. In the central reserve stack area each subject group has its own working space. The senior librarian-in-charge has a small office immediately to the rear of the readers' information counter and is readily available for consultation by his staff or for the private interviewing of readers. In the general lending and reference library area, as opposed to the popular area, seating and tables will be designed for study use. Periodicals will be housed in this area and the microfilm collection and reader, as well as maps and plans, will be available for consultation under counter staff control. Special collections such as the music and gramophone record library are housed in separate departments. I regret the necessity for this, as I should prefer to have these collections in areas opening off from the main public room.

The arrangement of the bookstocks is designed to facilitate the movement of the reader in accordance with his level of interest. As the interest of the reader becomes more specific or purposive, the incentive to move towards more specialised facilities arises naturally and the risk of frustration is reduced to the minimum.

In branch libraries a less elaborate arrangement is, of course, necessary. In one branch library which has been adapted and in our new branch library the charging and discharging counter has been removed from the main lending room. The bookstock is arranged on the open plan to allow provision of informal seating and tables and the focal point of the room is the librarian's information desk manned by the Bibliographical Division staff. This desk is specifically designed for branch library use and incorporates catalogues and quick reference shelves externally, while within providing suitable working space for the staff. The readers are obliged to go to the desk for everything they are likely to require, so that they are brought to the assistant on duty who is in a position to offer assistance without embarrassment to the reader. Our experience does suggest that by removing the charging counter in this way and substituting a professionally staffed desk, the number of inquiries from readers is stepped up considerably. The provision of a readers' advisory desk in the conventional lending library arrangement is not so successful—largely, I think, because there is more than one focal point in the room and some readers can be confused as to the purpose of each, and if not sure of themselves prefer not to seek assistance. A point which I think is worth mentioning in connection with the information desks is that we always refer to them as the 'librarian's desk' and each has a notice showing the designation and name of the librarian-in-charge. I have done this for two reasons;

readers, at least those in a predominantly working class borough, like to feel that they can approach the senior person in charge, and their attitude to the work of a librarian is likely then to be based on the service obtained from the professional staff.

Reference to the bibliographical collection has been made and I have described it as the major working tool. The subject specialisation arrangement quickly reveals the need for the best bibliographical collection that the library can afford, for it stimulates a better service, which in turn stimulates a higher level of inquiry from readers. We now spend almost as much on bibliographies as we spend on specifically reference books.

With the considerable delegation of authority which obtains in our system of organisation, it is essential for me to retain some overall control of its working, especially in the matter of book provision.

So far as day-to-day adjustment between the two divisions is concerned, the two senior officers settle these themselves. Proposed long term changes in staff must be referred to me and are usually dealt with at a periodical conference with my deputy and the other senior officers. This conference also acts as the final coordinating body. In each library and work unit the senior professional officer on duty takes overall responsibility, and as the location of these officers is reasonably continuous this general kind of responsibility is also continuous.

In matters of book provision the subject groups are directly responsible to me. The Administration Division maintains book stock records which assist me in allocating book funds to the groups. Each group maintains a simple running ledger of its book fund commitments, and at roughly quarterly intervals I adjust their financial allocations if necessary. I retain control of a substantial reserve amount in the book fund which is available to meet unexpected demands or to provide additional funds for special stock revision activity in any of the subject fields.

The subject groups have considerable discretion in the purchase of books, but prepare desiderata lists for all the more important items, which they discuss with me before purchase.

On the principle that it is easier to criticise other people's work than it is to criticise one's own, my deputy and I are constantly watching the effect of book purchases and stock adjustments, including the distribution of books as between libraries.

I should like to mention the book provision techniques which we are developing, but these need another paper to describe. They are intended to ensure that every interest among our readers receives a fully balanced representation and that each is continuously under review.

There still remains a number of problems to solve of which perhaps the most important at the present time are the physical arrangements in the central library building and the proper integration of the branch libraries into the scheme as a whole. The one will be met by the erection of a new building, and the other is a matter of continued experiment.

I cannot conclude without emphasising that the introduction of subject specialisation demands a completely fresh approach to every aspect of library organisation. I have not as yet fully considered all of its practical consequences, but the kind of question it does raise is, for example, whether or not the public catalogue as we have known it recedes in importance in favour of bibliographical aids to readers. Would the money spent on elaborate catalogues be better spent on a wide range of select bibliographies? I must leave such questions for future experience and, perhaps, for you to ponder.

As the result, however, of five years experience in a gradual change-over to the new principle of organisation, I am more than ever convinced that subject specialisation is the key to a new level of service and to the fullest use of our professional staffs.

REFERENCE
1 McCLELLAN, A. W: 'Service in depth'. *Library world*, April 1950. (See chapter 3.)

6: *Professional work for professional librarians*

A NUMBER of years ago Dr Savage analysed the operations performed by the staff of a public library and came to the conclusion that those which demanded a degree of professional training amounted to about one-third of the whole. In the United States and in this country, where the division of duties as between professional and non-professional has been applied effectively in recent years, experience confirms Dr Savage's earlier conclusion. It follows that when the different categories of work are allocated somewhat haphazardly over professional and non-professional staffs alike, the most economic distribution of duties is less easy to assess, and consequently is less likely to be achieved. At the same time the investment, which professional training surely is for the individual and society, is dissipated. The dispersion of activities over a variety of tasks, some of which are not essentially professional in character, leads to loss of personal interest and, possibly, lower status. There are, however, certain considerations of particular importance at the present time, which strengthen the case for a proper division of duties. If library service is to survive present day economic pressures, the organisation of duties so as to secure the maximum utilisation of resources is essential. It is only from the increased ' productivity ' brought about by such means that improved reward for professional work is likely to be obtained. The continuous development which is vital to any activity, if it is to adapt itself to changing conditions, needs a wider knowledge and a deeper perception of its possibilities, and will more readily be brought about if the trained librarian concentrates on work which calls for the exercise of his special skills and perceptions.

The soundness of a theoretical thesis seldom impresses the British librarian. The important question becomes ' Is it practicable? ', which resolves itself into two questions: is the division of duties required practicable, and is the staff available adequate to carry it out? Most of the operations in a library involve a combination of professional and clerical or semi-clerical activities. A careful analysis of all the operations is necessary, and provided a proper touchstone of assessment for segregating the professional part of these activities is adopted, it is not a difficult task. The unique features of librarianship are the knowledge and exploitation of books. The technical processes, such as classification and cataloguing, are subordinate to but part of these functions. It is a professional activity to select and recommend the purchase of books. The clerical work of recording recommendations is of course inseparable from the making of them, but the whole operation of ordering the books, checking the invoice, accessioning, etc is a clerical operation which can be carried out readily by non-professional staff. Most of the library operations can be as easily dealt with. Apart from the advantage of enabling the professional staffs to concentrate on professional work, with the consequent possibilities of development and refinement of their techniques, the concentration of clerical-administrative work which results permits the introduction of labour-saving methods and equipment, thereby improving the economy of resources. The practical division of duties along these lines does not require that it should be pushed to the theoretical extreme in every instance. There will be marginal difficulties, but these are surprisingly few and are resolved with a little applied commonsense.

If it is accepted that the division of duties is not, in itself difficult, then the criticism is sometimes made that in particular circumstances it is not practicable because insufficient professional staff is available. This may be due either to the fact that the proportion of professional staff is insufficient, or because the size of the library is inadequate to support the staff required. The mastery of circumstances is the administrator's continuing problem. To use them as a justification for inaction is hardly responsible. The lack of an adequate proportion of professional staff may often be overcome through a rationalisation of non-professional duties. Once the analysis of operations has been carried out, a reduction in the time required for non-professional duties may be obtained by the elimination of unnecessary routines, the centralisation of as many routines as possible, thereby permitting a degree of mechanisation, and by the introduction of analytical timesheets which are based on the principle of allocating staff to required points by the hour instead of by the day or the week. A combination of these arrangements may well afford the possibility of savings on non-professional staff which can be used for the employment of more professional staff. Should the foregoing prove inadequate it is still possible and advantageous to redeploy the duties so as to reduce the amount of non-professional work carried out by the professional staff. But if this is the best that can be done, then either the total staff available is inadequate whatever basis of organisation is used, or, what is more likely, the size of the library authority itself is inadequate.

A system of differentiation between professional and non-professional work is likely to produce two broad divisions in the organisation of the library system, a bibliographical division and a general administrative division. A reorganisation to such an extent will create its own problems and will in its initial stages give rise to some difficulties. Perhaps its outstanding problem is the new division of responsibility which is entailed. In each division responsibility for method and policy is self-contained and works through the various levels within the division. But coordination of work is necessary, and this is achieved through consultation between officers at the same level in the respective divisions. If difficulties occur at one level, the succeeding levels are brought in as required with the chief acting as final arbiter. This arrangement only differs from the conventional one to the extent that consultation has to take place between the two divisions at each level. While the so-called 'vertical responsibility' is thus taken care of, it leaves the question of 'horizontal responsibility' to be dealt with. By this is meant, 'Who takes overall responsibility within one unit or workplace when personnel of both divisions are engaged?'. The practical solution is to place the responsibility upon the senior professional officer on duty in the unit or workplace. These changes in the approach to responsibility may cause some initial confusion, but with habit and use the position becomes clarified.

The danger that there may be lack of variety and interest in the work for juniors aspiring to a professional career can arise in the conventional organisation of staff, but it is one which needs to be specially guarded against when a division of professional and non-professional duties exists. Present national policies of recruitment and training are not designed to encourage the recruitment of juniors specifically for professional work, as is the case in other professions. The danger can be greatly minimised, however, through a number of measures such as a good scheme of inservice training, use of a central pool of staff for a variety of near professional tasks (and, incidentally, this fits in with the adoption of analytical time-sheets), temporary upgrading to professional duties of promising assistants during periods of sickness, holidays, etc, rapid promotion on obtaining basic qualifications, and creation of responsible posts on the general duties side, *eg* senior general assistants, working in close contact with professional staff.

Professional exclusiveness can also be a danger. The division of duties must be applied with some commonsense. Petty attitudes as to what falls into one division or the other must be treated with the scorn they deserve. The true profession demands some sense of dedication, a measure of humility and modesty, and a willingness to turn to any task which needs to be done. The professional owes a responsibility to the general staff in expressing such characteristics in his day to day relations with them. The professional must set the example by displaying what is ultimately the basis of all professions—service to humanity. In the long run, a profession is judged by its results and by the quality of its members, not by its claims and assertions of status.

7: *Accessibility and other problems of book provision*

I HAVE TRIED to show on a previous occasion[1] that successful book provision results from the integration of three factors which govern individual reader transactions—namely, readers, books and accessibility.

The importance of relating the books provided to the readers using the library is, perhaps, self-evident. It is generally accepted too that it is important that readers should be able to get the books they want as quickly as possible, ideally of course, at the time the books are required. Yet this aspect of book provision does not receive the attention it deserves. Is there not at times an ambivalent attitude taken towards the desire of the reader to get the book he wants when he wants it? Having done our best to assess the kinds of readers using the library and to provide suitable books for them, and, in addition, having spent considerable time and money in classifying and cataloguing the books so that they may be readily located, are we not inclined to feel that we have done all that can be reasonably expected? Does not the devotion of more of our resources to ensuring that the reader actually gets the book he wants when he wants it savour of ' spoonfeeding '? We do provide ' open-access '; isn't, the rest rather up to the reader?

On the other hand, surely, the whole object of the careful matching of books and readers is to bring about as many successful marriages of them as possible. It is this business of the successful marrying of the right book with the right reader that I want to examine. But particularly that aspect concerned with bringing the two together at the right time.

Between the fact of the existence of a particular book and a reader's need of it, lies a range of possibility of the reader getting the book, within a period acceptable to him, varying from immediate satisfaction to never at all. The book may be on the shelf, in a reserve stack, in the hands of another reader, set aside as involved in some library process, or in some other library, perhaps even in some other country. In other

72

words the reader's access to the book can vary considerably. To describe this aspect of book provision I use the word *accessibility*.

Accessibility is the achilles heel of the public library system. Getting the book to the reader at the time he wants it is one of our greatest practical difficulties. A systematic examination of the problem is desirable if improved techniques are to be developed and evaluated. In fact these may well be suggested by such an examination.

The degrees of accessibility of books to readers at the time they are ready to borrow them conveniently fall into the following phases:

Immediate choice—which denotes that the book which is required or which is suitable is actually on the shelves when the reader requires it.

Internal locations—which denotes that the book is nominally in the stock of the library system but is not immediately available. The book may be on loan to another reader or located elsewhere in the library system, *eg* at a branch library, at binding, pending withdrawal from stock, in reserve stock, somewhere in the accessioning process or even on staff loan.

Bibliographical and external locations: which denotes the use of bibliographies to establish the existence of the book leading to external locations, *eg* sources for books outside the library system, *eg* interlending schemes, book trade, legal, medical and drama subscription libraries, etc.

Clearly, the maximum amount of satisfaction to readers will be possible if they are able to get suitable books in the phase of ' immediate choice ', *ie* when they actually visit the library. It cannot be overstressed that the field of immediate choice for the reader consists of the books actually on the shelves at the time of his visit. At any given moment about 95 percent of the readers interested in a given subject will have books on loan on that subject. Naturally, these books on loan will tend to be those which are most desirable to the individual readers. If each reader at the time of his visit is to get the best chance of satisfaction, then it will not be sufficient to ensure that the stock held by the library is adequate in range and levels in each subject. Book provision policy will need to ensure that there is continuously available *on the shelves* an adequate choice in range and levels of books in each subject. The important question is not ' Is there a copy of this book in stock? ' but, ' What chances has a reader of getting this book when he wants it, or when it would meet his particular need? '. To say that the book may be reserved for the reader is not an adequate answer, if only because frequently the reader is unaware that a particular book is what he wants until he has had an opportunity of actually examining it.

The regular inspection of books on the shelves is therefore essential. In this way a clear picture of a reader's *immediate* choice in a subject can be acquired. This regular inspection is best ensured if it forms part of a systematic stock revision process such as I have outlined in another paper.[1] Where the staff is organised into subject divisions or departments it is particularly helpful too if the approximate number of readers in each subject is known. A regular count of the number of books on loan in each subject, say four times a year, will give a practical enough figure for readers. These measures, together with continuous watching of reservations and requests, will reveal that books on some aspects of a subject are seldom immediately available, and, similarly, books at some levels of approach to a subject will not be available. Such shortcomings must be met by appropriate additional books. Within each subject will also be noted certain titles which are seldom, if ever, to be found on the shelves. These should be subjected to a careful process of duplication. The object should be to see that one copy of the title is regularly available. One of the dangers of duplicating copies, however, is that it is difficult to avoid occasions when more than one copy is on the shelves. Readers are apt to be irritated by seeing several copies of books on the shelves, considering perhaps, that the money spent on the duplication might have been better spent on other books. It is desirable, therefore, to devise an arrangement whereby a duplicate copy is shelved only if no other copy is on the shelf. In British libraries it is not easy to make such an arrangement, which will at the same time avoid the possibility that duplicates will not be shelved at all. The solution is a simple one and is widely used in German and other continental libraries, namely to utilise the lower shelves of bookstacks as cupboards in which duplicate copies are stored out of sight. At regular intervals, preferably daily, the duplicate copies where necessary are placed on the open shelves immediately above. With the current tendency to raise the level of the lowest shelf in the bookstack, provision of such storage space would not be difficult to incorporate in the bookstack. The fact that our bookstack design seldom makes such provision indicates that the value of systematic duplication is not widely appreciated as yet.

The principal object in this phase, however, is a book provision policy based on the stock which is continuously available on the shelves with the careful duplication of certain titles as a part of that policy. If the policy is backed up by a high-level readers' advisory service which readers have learned to use freely and good guiding to shelves, then the degree of reader satisfaction of the phase of immediate choice will be greatly extended. In turn the work involved at the extended stages of accessibility, *ie* internal and external locations, will be correspondingly lessened.

Nevertheless, many readers will not obtain immediate satisfaction, if only because the resources of the library are inevitably limited. This will apply especially to readers who have specific titles in mind. The satisfaction of the reader will then depend on the efficiency of the library's bibliographical, reservation and request services.

Reservation and request systems constitute one of the least effective of public library techniques. In theory it should be simple to locate and set aside a specific book. A considerable amount of time is devoted to classification, cataloguing and accessioning, with a view to making location quick and easy, and yet how elusive is the individual book when required.

What are the basic needs of an effective reservation system? First undoubtedly, is a thorough appreciation throughout the library system that readers requests for books must receive a high priority. If the reader is needing attention when present in the library, we accept the need to drop whatever we may be doing to deal with him at once. Clearly, therefore, if we have been unable to give him an immediate satisfaction and his request has to be dealt with later it is even more essential to give his rapid satisfaction a high priority. Requests for the same title should be satisfied in strict order of receipt, and, when more than one copy is stocked utilising all the copies available in the system. How can one answer a reader who, having reserved a book in one library and having waited weeks for it, finds a copy on the shelves at another library in the system? How long should a reader be expected to wait before being notified that his book is available? In normal circumstances I would say that at the maximum it should not exceed more than two periods of loan, *ie* four to six weeks. A system of automatically ordering extra copies of heavily reserved titles is necessary to meet such a target. The reservation organisation must also allow for the rapid location of the first available copies and their rapid transfer from one part of the library system to another.

In order to meet the need for a high degree of priority in dealing with reservations and requests and in view of the continuous need to make use of all available copies throughout a library system a central staff unit with full responsibility for location and transfer appears to be essential. A central staff unit would also be in a position to work closely with accessioning and bibliographical staffs, thus making easier the location of copies. It is also essential that all requests are dealt with in a continuous flow; at all stages they should be cleared within 24 hours. Accumulations permitted at any stage play havoc with the time factor between date of request and ultimate satisfaction. Finally, and I think the crucial requirement, is a system of recording the movements of individual books so that their up-to-date location is simple and speedy.

The main book records are of course, the accessions or book stock record and the catalogues. Their preparation and maintenance is both costly and laborious. It is difficult to keep them either accurate or fully up-to-date and for these reasons they are frequently unreliable for the location of individual titles. The rapid reproduction of catalogue entries has received much attention in recent years. It has appeared to me however that the chief problem arising from the provision of catalogues lies in the amount of sheer physical labour involved in the deadly task of filing, withdrawing and amending entries. It is also a task that demands some professional qualification and experience and appropriate staff have to be used to do it. The easier it is to reproduce catalogue entries the greater is the temptation to increase the number of copies of the catalogue—an extra copy is always handy—what can be overlooked is the consequent serious increase in the work of maintenance and the danger that the catalogues will not be reliable and up-to-date. On the other hand if there is need for reference to a catalogue at the central library the smaller book resources of branch libraries justifies the use of a catalogue to an even greater extent, especially from the point of view of the branch professional staff.

It occurred to me that what was needed was a means whereby an entry could be reproduced and transmitted almost simultaneously to the point of inquiry as required. Such a means would reproduce only those entries or the portions of information needed which were actually asked for. It is perhaps a surprising fact that while a catalogue contains several entries for every book held in stock, the number of books which are actually the subject of catalogue reference is quite a small proportion of the total stock.

Recently there has been introduced a piece of electronic equipment which does almost precisely what is required. It is known as Desk-Fax and is based on the same principle as telex (as used in Manchester and increasingly in other libraries) but with the advantages that it is simpler, can be used by anybody who can write, is relatively inexpensive, and can be installed into a private telephone circuit without going through any form of public exchange. Briefly, it consists of an instrument, about the size of a portable typewriter, known as a transceiver (because the same instrument both transmits and receives messages). A transceiver, connected by private telephone wire to the other transceivers in the system, is installed at each inquiry or message point. To send a message, which can be hand written or typed, it is necessary only to insert into the machine a slip of paper (about 6″ × 4″ in size) containing the message, press a button and the machine will immediately commence to reproduce a facsimile of the message on the transceiver stationed at the distant point selected. The whole of the message area on the message form takes about two minutes to reproduce. If however, the message consists of small quantities of information such as will be contained in one or two lines of writing, as for example, the author, title number and location of a book, the time taken for reproduction is reduced proportionally to the amount of space on the form which is utilised. It is possible therefore for the kind of information with which we are mostly concerned to be transmitted from one library to another in as little time as 12 to 20 seconds—which is close to being simultaneous. On completion of a message the transceiver leaves it in a position to be retransmitted without removal or rewriting, to another station. It is only necessary then to press a button to direct the original message to a further station as desired. This can be repeated as required. Thus, it is possible to transmit details of a single book to say six libraries in no more than two or three minutes. It will be noted how useful this can be for the tracing of first available copies of books. Incidentally the message transmitting form can be of ordinary paper and can be printed in any style suitable for particular purposes.

The installation of the Desk-Fax system throughout the library system offers the means required for an excellent locations index, which can be kept up-to-date remarkably easily, and which makes the task of locating the first available copy of a book much speedier. It enables a considerable simplification of book records to be organised with a consequent saving in time and labour.

At Tottenham, where I have installed the system, it is necessary to have only two copies of the main book entry against the former nine copies. One master main entry catalogue is maintained at the central library and is the only catalogue which involves the insertion, withdrawal or amendment of entries. It also serves as the accessions or stock record, no separate accessions record being necessary. It is not even necessary to maintain a register of accession numbers, these being obtained from information which is contained already in each individual book and which in fact can nearly always be obtained from the appropriate entry in the *British national bibliography.*

The procedure for maintaining the master catalogue and locations index is simple. As mentioned before two manuscript cards are made out for each book. One is a desiderata and order card, which is made out for every book added to stock. Starting as a desiderata card, it is used for compiling book orders after approval of purchase. When the order is placed the card is inserted into the master catalogue where it is readily distinguishable by virtue of its colour, which is in contrast with the catalogue cards, and by the fact that it is made to project one eighth of an inch above them. The other card is the manuscript main entry catalogue card, which is inserted into the master catalogue after the book is processed. At the same time the corresponding desiderata and order card is withdrawn and is available for compiling book lists, statistics and regional entries. Thus the master catalogue contains not only the entries for books in stock, but entries for books on order but not yet received. This arrangement enables requested books which are on order to be chased up and dealt with out of turn. Amendment and withdrawal of entries is effected by using the charging card of the book concerned. The charging card is rubber stamped on the reverse, where suitable instructions are marked, sent to the central library, where the locations staff amend the master catalogue accordingly.

All enquiries for book information arising from reservations and requests are transmitted by the Desk-Fax installation and facsimile transcripts of the information from the master catalogue are sent back to the points of inquiry. All copies in stock are indicated, and if a copy is not available at the originating library, the central locations unit can transmit a request by Desk-Fax for the first available copy to be reported. A feature of the Desk-Fax which is very valuable in this connection is the fact that both sender and receiver have facsimile copies of messages sent. A useful ancillary piece of equipment has recently been designed which is well adapted to the system I have described. The conventional card cabinet when housing a large central catalogue can be very cumbersome, and inconvenient to use. The new catalogue card container, ' the card-master ', is so designed that all cards can be quickly brought to the position of the assistant referring to it and who does not need to move from a fixed seated position. At the same time it is possible for other staff to work on the catalogue without difficulty.

Depending on local line conditions the maximum range of Desk-Fax transmission is 5 to 10 miles. In library areas therefore, where libraries are at greater distances Desk-Fax would not prove suitable, or economic. Telex would then be the answer. Buckinghamshire County Library have for this reason adopted telex to operate such a system. Three of their libraries already have telex installed and it is intended progressively to extend the area covered. Other county libraries are also considering similar schemes.

With the introduction of this electronic device the opportunity arises for the complete centralisation of the reservation and request organisation, with the exception of the actual location of books on the shelf, in the issue records or as returned at the various libraries. A central location unit under a responsible assistant can be set up to locate first copies available, to direct copies to the requesting library and to ensure that requests are dealt with in strict rotation over the system as a whole. Such a system needs to be backed up by a frequent delivery service, preferably daily between all the libraries.

The central location unit can then appropriately deal with requests which fall into the last phase of accessibility, namely, bibliographical and external locations. Books which are not available from stock have to be borrowed or purchased. So the central locations staff take responsibility for all regional requests and loans, and in association with the bibliographical staff deal with books which have to be purchased or otherwise obtained outside the system to meet reservations or requests.

In this last phase of accessibility the importance of the best bibliographical collection cannot be overstressed. A method of readily ascertaining the number of readers in any subject field, to which I referred earlier, helps in a rapid decision as to whether to buy or to borrow.

No matter how efficient the organisation for bringing the book to the reader as quickly as possible, there are factors outside our control which will cause delay. The reader cannot be expected to appreciate our difficulties, but he will appreciate being informed when delay is likely. At all stages of dealing with requests therefore it is good policy to ensure that the reader is notified of possible delay in meeting his request. This should be an automatic routine.

The question of the accessibility of books to readers as a factor in reader satisfaction needs considerably more thought and examination than can be afforded in one paper. But what I have said so far immediately brings to mind a further question of basic importance to the kind of service we give to readers.

Is the provision of the public catalogue in the general lending library necessary? Consider some of the changes which have taken place since the public catalogue was considered only second in importance to the books in a library:

a) The number of readers in relation to the total book stock has increased enormously—the turnover of books in stock has correspondingly increased, so that the catalogue no longer reflects a semi-permanent collection of books, the greater part of which is always available on the shelves. Now on average one third of the bookstock is always out—in some sections as much as 90 percent of the books will be continuously out. The catalogue is no longer a reliable guide to what is immediately available.

b) While the central core of the regular readership may be satisfied with the books immediately available, there is an increasing margin of readers whose horizons stretch well beyond the range of the bookstock of a particular library. The range of interests has grown and so has their depth.

c) The catalogue was the major bibliographical tool for readers. But with the growth in range and depth of interests the bibliography of the literature, rather than the stock, is needed to meet them.

These changes in the relationships of the catalogue to the reader are fully evidenced by the growth of interlending, the increase in bibliographical collections in public libraries and the growth of professional assistance to readers. For these reasons the development of professional assistance to readers is supplanting the public catalogue as second only to books in the library.

The public catalogue is now, surely, having a restrictive effect on readers and on the professional staffs? The use of the catalogue as the prime source of reference limits the horizon of the reader to the book-stock and deters the librarian from exploring the bibliography of the literature, so that he may ascertain more precisely what will best suit the needs of the reader. At the same time the incentive to know books and their bibliography is reduced, thereby reducing too, the value of the librarian to the reader.

Naturally, a number of readers like using a catalogue and would be reluctant to see it eliminated. If one questions closely the few readers who like to use the catalogue one finds their answers reduce to such considerations as: Has the library got a particular book in stock? What sort of books are there in particular subjects?

Closely related to that last question is the desire simply to peruse with a view to coming across something which looks interesting. The last two considerations involve the use of the catalogue as a bibliography —*ie* as a guide to various fields of literature. The concern is not particularly with whether or not particular books are in stock, that comes at a later stage, when, as a result of his perusal of the catalogue he decides he would like to read a specific title. At that point he is really concerned not with whether it is in stock, but with whether it is immediately available. That, surely, too, is precisely the position of the reader who asks the first question, *ie* 'Has the library a particular book in stock?'.

If the reader finds that the book is not immediately available but *is* in stock he will feel that in some degree the book is still accessible to him and may continue to look for it or even ask for it. But if he learns from the catalogue that it is not in stock he may well feel that its degree of accessibility is nil; and will not bother with it any more unless he has a strong desire to have it.

We know, however, that the book may be much more accessible than he realises. With our inter-lending schemes we could possibly obtain it fairly quickly, we could buy it, or it might even have been purchased already but not have been entered in the catalogue, or it might actually be on order but not yet received.

We also know that if the book is shown as in stock, the measure of accessibility which the reader imagines he has to the book is much higher than we know it to be in fact. We know, but he doesn't, that the book may be at the binder's, may be in the hands of a recalcitrant reader who invariably takes months to return a book, may be on 3 months' loan to another library, may have been withdrawn but the catalogue entry has not, and, of course, may well be lost, which we don't discover until we start to hunt for it. We could also know that the catalogue is only about 50 percent accurate because it is so difficult to maintain.

The bibliographical needs of the reader are surely better served by a profusion of short introductory booklists backed by fuller booklists, all evaluative if possible. These should also introduce the reader to the major bibliographical tools available. Better still, and additionally, condition the reader to use the continuously available professional assistance of librarians who know their books and the ways of bibliography as few laymen do. The chances of the reader learning to know which particular book will meet his needs or satisfy his interest best will surely be much greater through such means than an inexpert perusal of the catalogue could produce. Do not forget the scores of rules you had to learn before you could properly arrange a catalogue—what hope has the reader with such an instrument?

If the book is not immediately available, the reader is not genuinely interested in whether it is in stock, for this to him is only an indication of how quickly it might be available. Condition him to the idea that what is not immediately available will be obtained as quickly as possible. He'll not be worried where and how you get it but how soon. Don't condition him to the use of an instrument which can only give him false and limited notions of the possibilities of a good library service.

Study the problems of accessibility, devote as much attention to it as to the selection, classifying and cataloguing of books, and your reader will take it for granted that you can get the right book for him at the right time, or any rate, at very nearly the right time.

REFERENCE

1 McClellan, A W: 'New concepts of service'. *Library Association record,* August 1956. (See chapter 4.)

8: *Systematic stock control in public libraries*

THE TWO ASPECTS OF BOOK PROVISION: In a particular library the principal task, namely, book provision, is pursued within a context of limited physical and financial resources. The library will be incapable of shelving more than an infinitesimal proportion of existing literature, so that the readers' needs may outstrip the immediate potential of the library. Hence questions arise as to what fields of literature are to be represented in the book stock, what ratios of representation should be aimed at as between the various fields, and what degrees of accessibility to books are to be afforded to readers? The criteria for answering these questions must derive from the underlying objectives of the library, but to ensure that the book stock conforms to these objectives within the limits of resources is an administrative problem involving the organisation of the library and the use of appropriate methods and techniques.

The book stock tends continuously to deteriorate through its exhaustion by the readers, physical wear and tear and the obsolescence of individual titles. The readership is changing through the influx of new readers, the loss of readers and the mobility of readers across the fields of literature. Accessibility is varied by virtue of the need to limit the immediately available stock to the open-shelf capacity of the library and the consequent setting up of concentrated storage areas which reduce the level of accessibility.

The complexity of the factors involved suggests that the operations essential to effective book provision can be conveniently recognised as falling into two categories. On the one hand are the operations concerned with upholding the basic objectives, that is to say, the correct distribution of books as between the various fields of literature in accordance with the varying needs of readers, the maximisation of the readers' accessibility to books, the minimisation of the deterioration in the book stock, the avoidance of subjective discrimination against individual or groups of readers, and overall conformity to the resources available. This whole group of operations might be designated the 'logistical' aspect of book provision.

On the other hand are the operations concerned with the assessment of individual books to ensure that an appropriate bibliographical balance is continuously maintained in each field of literature represented in the book stock, that individual reader requirements can be met, and that overall the book stock does not depart unduly from its logistical requirements. In contrast this whole group of operations might be designated the 'bibliographical' aspect of book provision.

Whereas the logistical operations will be concerned with the numbers of books which, desirably, may need to be stocked in a given field of literature, the bibliographical operations will be concerned with the individual titles and their duplication, if necessary, in that field. It follows that these two kinds of operations will utilise quite different principles and techniques to achieve their objectives. The bibliographical operations are essentially matters of personal judgement and will necessarily be based on training, knowledge and experience related to single units, whether they be books or readers. The logistical operations, however, because they are concerned with the condition and characteristics of *classes or groups* of books and readers, can utilise statistical and mathematical concepts and techniques.

The operations which fall under the logistical aspect of book provision have received little attention. It is this aspect, and particularly methods and techniques related to it that I am concerned to develop in this paper.

THE 'SCALE OF ACCESSIBILITY'

The first point to note is that operations will be geared to 'provision', regardless of whether what is needed is immediately available or not. Provision is affected by three conditions of accessibility: *immediate accessibility*—in which access is immediately possible, and comprises books on the open-shelf space at any one time; *limited accessibility*—in which access may be obtained on request, and comprises books temporarily withdrawn from circulation or placed permanently in reserve; *deferred accessibility*—in which access is deferred over varying periods of time, and comprises books currently on loan to other readers, books out of circulation and not normally on the library premises, books obtainable by purchase only, books obtainable from subscription libraries, or books obtainable from interlending sources.

The basic problem becomes one of placing books on a 'scale of accessibility '. Only the reader can be the ultimate judge as to which end of the scale the book should be placed. Our aim must be to stock those books which are likely to have the greatest use, while at the same time perfecting the machinery for securing those books which cannot be stocked because their potential use is lower than shelf capacity will accept, or otherwise are not immediately available.

In adopting the readers' use of books as the principal criterion in assembling the stock, the danger arises that the wide range of minority interests in the readership will be ignored, or, at best, inadequately represented. On the other hand, a subjective discrimination between readers is even less desirable. The readers themselves, however, do operate a form of differentiation, and one which is not only acceptable among themselves but is regarded by them as perfectly natural. They expect to find in the library books which cater for their particular interests. They accept also that other readers having quite different interests shall be similarly catered for. The behaviour of the readers in this respect suggests the use of the variety of interests present in the readership as the principle of differentiation within the book stock. If we group the stock into a series of *interest categories* and we try and ensure that within the resources available no individual interest category is over-represented at the expense of other interest categories, the principle of a ' scale of accessibility ' can be operated within the context of single categories only. The effect of this arrangement will be that the use of a book in one interest category will not be evaluated by comparison with the use of books in other categories. Thus a book falling into an interest category which continuously attracts a relatively small number of readers will almost certainly have a history of use smaller than a book falling into a category which continuously attracts a large readership. The scale of accessibility principle being applied independently to each of the categories, the book likely to enjoy a smaller use could command as high or even a higher priority for inclusion as the book likely to enjoy a much greater use. Accordingly, records of books and readers will relate to fields of interest. The division of the stock into groups of interests may be based on an existing classification scheme such as Dewey, but the number of groups to be employed will depend on whether the ultimate records are to be processed manually or by computer. Manual processing could cope with about 150 categories, while computer processing could cope with a much larger number. The essential point is that the categories should reflect discrete fields of readers' interests.

Having settled the interest categories into which the stock is to be divided, how are they to be proportionately represented? The key to the problem again lies in the concept of the scale of accessibility. When a book is on loan it can be said to have a deferred accessibility so far as the reader in the library is concerned. Readers in all categories, whether these be large or small, will have an approximately equal degree of deferred accessibility to the books on loan in those categories. It is only when the reader has immediate accessibility to the books, *ie* when he visits the library, that serious inequality in range of choice is likely to arise. What principally concerns the reader is the range of choice available to him on his visit to the library. A way has to be found, therefore, whereby in each interest category there will be a large enough stock of books to ensure that a balance remains on the shelves which will be sufficient in number and utility to afford a reasonable choice for the individual reader. The stock in active circulation will consist of 'books on loan' and 'books on the shelves'. I refer to these respectively as, the 'loan component' and the 'shelf component' of the stock. If then, the range of immediate choice is the main concern of the reader, it is the representation of the shelf components of all the interest categories which becomes the significant problem.

The shelf components of each interest category cannot in total exceed the shelf capacity of the library. How, in spite of the differing numbers of readers attracted to the interest categories, is the shelf stock to be apportioned between them fairly but not wastefully? We could divide the total shelf stock by the number of interest categories, so that whatever his broad field of interest each reader would have the same number of books to choose from. Suppose we have a shelf capacity of 15,000 volumes and say, 150 interest categories into which it has to be divided, then each category would be entitled to a shelf stock of 100 volumes. But some interest categories will attract perhaps only five readers continuously, while other categories will attract hundreds of readers. In the former case the readers would necessarily have such a large number of books to choose from that many would remain unread, and in order to maintain a flow of new material from year to year many books would have to be withdrawn unused. In the latter case readers would exhaust the books available very rapidly. Obviously the waste of resources involved could be avoided to better purpose by augmenting the categories where books would be read.

We could divide the shelf stock by the total number of readers and allocate this number for each reader continuously using an interest category, assuming that we had a ready means of assessing this number. If our shelf capacity were 15,000 volumes and the total number of readers was, say, 10,000, then each interest category would be entitled to a shelf stock of $1\frac{1}{2}$ volumes per reader attracted to the category. An interest category attracting say 5 readers would have a shelf stock of, say, 8 volumes; an interest category attracting 100 readers would have a shelf stock of 150 volumes. Clearly this situation would be unsatisfactory, because the readers in the smaller category would find a totally inadequate range of choice on the shelves. Furthermore, if we assume that an average rate of borrowing per reader is say, 15 volumes per annum, then each reader in the smaller category will have exhausted the stock in less than nine months.

THE PRINCIPLE OF REPRESENTATION BY SQUARE ROOT

We need, therefore, to find a principle of representation for the shelf stock which will avoid the extremes of wastefulness, in the form of unused books, or an undue restriction of choice in the smaller interest categories. We know that large groups of readers are attracted to a comparatively small number of fields of interest, as for example, biography and novels; but we know too that there are many minority interests among the readership, and we accept the need to ensure that these minority interests receive adequate representation.

In order to minimise confusion at a later stage it will be useful at this point to consider the significance attached to the term ' loan component '. It is that portion of the books comprising an interest category which happen at any particular time to be on loan to readers. Unless readers are limited to retaining one book at a time, the number of books on loan is not synonymous with the number of readers using the stock at that time. The actual readers within an interest category will differ from one another in the frequency with which they read books, in the number of books they will borrow at one time, and at different times, and in the persistence with which they will continue to read books in the category. The sum or total effect of all these variations in use of books within the category is expressed in the number of books which are shown to be continuously on loan. A count of books on loan on the same day will reflect all the aspects of use by the actual readers in terms of the number of books required *at that particular time,* to satisfy those aspects of use.

For example, to take one aspect of use, the numbers of books borrowed at a time: if the number of books recorded as on loan is 10 volumes, it may represent 10 readers with one book each, or two readers, one with two books and one with eight books on loan. With each of these possibilities the number of books required by the readers is ten and if we are to afford an adequate representation in the stock we must allow for at least that number. So that for our logistical operations the number of books on loan, *ie* the 'loan component', is of more value than knowing the number of readers actually involved. Whether, within one interest category, what is involved is one reader needing 10 books or 10 readers needing one book each, the range of choice in numerical terms is the same. This is not the case however, when the stock is being viewed for its bibliographical content. But the content of the stock is a matter for the bibliographical aspect of our operations, and we are not concerned with these at the moment.

To return to the principle of adequate proportional representation of the interest categories in the book stock, we have found that methods using directly proportional representation are not satisfactory. If, however, we accept that the loan component of each interest category can be regarded for this purpose as reflecting use by the current readership, a practical compromise can be achieved by use of square root. By taking a count of the books on loan for each category at a given time, we have a number which is the loan component of the stock in circulation. The square root for each number is taken from a table or via a computer. The square roots obtained from all the interest category loan components are totalled and then each individual square root is calculated as a percentage of that total. The shelf stock for each interest category is calculated by expressing its loan component percentage as a percentage of the total open shelf capacity of the library. The effect of this method of arriving at desirable proportions between the categories is to introduce a controlled bias in favour of the smaller interest categories. It increases the representation of these categories very substantially, but it does so without unduly reducing the range of choice in the larger interest categories. It minimises wasteful provision in the smaller categories whilst avoiding the danger that these categories will be overwhelmed by the demands made upon the larger categories. The total desired circulating stock for each interest category is obtained by adding together the two components, *ie*

the loan component—the highest count of books on loan taken from a series of counts;

the shelf component—the square root of the loan component as a proportion of the total of all square roots of the loan components multiplied by the library's shelf capacity.

By recalculating these proportions at intervals it is possible to cater for the changing interests of the readership by varying the circulating stock accordingly. It should be noted also that although the total shelf stock remains static under all conditions, its turnover may increase, the number of books on loan may increase, and the proportional representation of the interest categories within the stock may vary. The method will cope with all or any of these changes.

The quantitative basis of a desirable stock may be calculated in this way, and will ensure that all the interests of readers can be adequately represented within it. But the book stock cannot remain static either in quantity or in content. The continuous tendency of the book stock to fall away from the logistical pattern and the bibliographical standard calls for an equally continuous counter-action. The systematic revision of the book stock is at least as necessary as its systematic development. We may describe the counter-action as one of maintaining the logistical and bibliographical balances. To be effective, however, it is necessary to identify the factors which make for depreciation and to locate continuously those parts of the book stock where counter-action, for the time being, is most urgently called for.

DEPRECIATION FACTORS

We can say that depreciation takes two forms, quantitative and qualitative.

Quantitative depreciation arises from:

[i] Physical wear and tear.

[ii] The exhaustion of the existing stocks by the interested readers, *ie* the readers will have read all the books available in an interest category which they will want to read, irrespective of their intrinsic value or physical condition.

[iii] Excessive or inadequate stocks in particular interest categories due to changes in the interests of readers, inadequate revision or cumulated errors in accessions to the stock.

Qualitative depreciation arises from:

[i] The publication of better editions of existing works.

[ii] Publication of fresh works which incorporate fresh knowledge, developments, ideas or perceptions.

89

[iii] Publication of works restating and re-presenting previously diffused truths, ideas and knowledge in the contemporary idiom, or in a more imaginative, satisfying or effective form.

RATES OF DEPRECIATION

If we can devise methods of expressing these various types of depreciation in terms of rates or periods, we shall be in a position to determine the annual replacements needed to maintain the stock in all interest categories at desirable levels.

Potential issue life of stock:

The physical life of the stock may be expressed in terms of the number of issues it will bear. Estimates, based on practical tests, have shown that we may allow 60 issues for fiction titles and children's books, and, say, 75 issues for non-fiction titles as a reasonable life in each case. If we calculate the desired stock as indicated previously and multiply the resulting figure by the appropriate 'issue life factor', *ie* 60 or 75, we shall have an estimate of the total of potential issues to be expected from that stock. For example, if we suppose that in a fiction interest category the desired stock is estimated to be 400 volumes, then multiplying by the issue life factor of 60, we may expect the potential issue of the 400 volumes to be 24,000. Once the potential issue of the stock is known, then the period of its life can be assessed by dividing that figure by the actual or estimated number of issues which occur in one year.

If the annual issues in an interest category are divided by the highest number of a count of books on loan (the loan component of the count previously referred to) in a particular year, an 'issue rate factor' for the loan component is obtained. Thus, if the number of books on loan was the highest for the year and was, say, 100, and the issues in that category for the year were 1500, then the issue rate would be 1500 divided by 100 which is 15. Experience has shown that the issue rate factor does not vary much from year to year, so that it needs to be recalculated at infrequent intervals. It will also be found that the issue rate factor need be calculated for broad groups of related interest categories only, and not necessarily for each interest category. Interest categories within a main class will have very much the same issue rate factor.

Returning to our example of estimated potential issue life, *ie* 400 volumes estimated to have an issue life of 24,000, we will have found that the issue rate factor for novels is say 20. Assuming that the highest count of books on loan was say, 300, then the estimated annual issue for this category of novels would be 20×300 which is 6000. The potential issue life of the stock, as we have seen, is 24,000, and dividing this by 6000 equals 4, which means that the life of this stock can be expected to be 4 years. In this manner we can estimate the issue life of the stock in all the interest categories into which the stock is classified.

Reader exhaustion of stock:

The physical life of the stock is a factor of the number of issues the stock will bear, but the readers may exhaust the stock before it becomes physically useless. On the other hand, the physically useful life of the stock may not be sufficient to enable the readers to read all the books in the category.

If the readers in a category borrow an average of 15 books a year, then, if there is a stock of 60 books, each reader will on average take 4 years to read all 60 books.

To take the previous example, we said that the stock consisted of 400 novels, and that the average annual issue per reader was 20, so that a reader would take 20 years to read all the books in that category.

THE ANNUAL REPLACEMENT RATE

By a determination of the rates of depreciation to which the stock is subjected it is possible to estimate what number of books is needed annually to replenish the stock so as to maintain its quantitative levels. We have shown that there are two major factors at work making for the quantitative depreciation of the stock, and these we have described as the issue life of the stock and the reader exhaustion rate.

These depreciation rates relate only to forms of quantitative decline in the stock. But the maintenance of the desired quantitative levels will not necessarily take care of a possible qualitative decline resulting from bibliographical obsolescence.

In the great majority of interest categories, the renewal periods suggested by the issue life and reader exhaustion rates will be short enough to ensure that the bibliographical obsolescence of the stock can be taken care of through the normal book selection and revision operations. In instances where they will not do so, it is necessary at present to make use of an arbitrary period which will be short enough to ensure that the bibliographical condition of the stock is not allowed to deteriorate to a point where it becomes unsuitable in content for its readers.

The qualitative depreciation of the stock, which I refer to as its *obsolescence*, arises through the publication of improved editions of existing works, fresh works incorporationg fresh knowledge, developments, ideas, and perceptions; and works restating and representing previously diffused truths, ideas and knowledge in the contemporary idiom, or in a more imaginative, satisfying or effective form.

The rate of such obsolescence is not readily predictable. There are, however, some maximum limits, based on experience, which can be set. This is an area in which some research would enable us to be more precise, but for illustrative purposes I will use the following and will refer to them as the ' obsolescent rate ':

	Obsolescent rate
Children's books	5 years or 20 percent
Adult fiction	5 years or 20 percent
non-fiction	
science & technology	8 years or $12\frac{1}{2}$ percent
other	12 years or $8\frac{1}{3}$ percent

Determination of the annual replacement rate

We are now in a position by making use of these rates of depreciation, namely, issue life, reader exhaustion and obsolescence rates, to determine the annual replacement rate for the stock.

If we say that the annual replacement rate should be based on whichever of the three depreciation rates involves a shorter renewal period, we shall ensure that the other depreciation factors will have been allowed for as well. For this reason it will be found unnecessary to calculate all three forms of depreciation in respect of every interest category. The calculation of one will often be sufficient. The obsolescent rates are constant and thus are already known.

I can illustrate this point by quoting the rates obtaining for a popular fiction category and a non-fiction category : —

a) A popular fiction category had the following rates :

Issue life rate	3 years
Reader exhaustion rate	108 years

(In this category emphasis on replacement of individual titles will be called for.)

b) A non-fiction category, child psychology, has the following rates :

Issue life rate	22 years
Reader exhaustion rate	5 years

(In this category emphasis on provision of new titles will be called for.)

It will be seen, therefore, that the annual replacement rate for each of these categories will be, in the first category 3 years, and in the second 5 years. As in both instances the appropriate obsolescent rate is higher, it can be ignored.

The effect of these replacement rates is that in calculating the book fund requirements for the next year, allowance must be made for the replacement of one third of the stock in the first category and of one fifth of the stock in the second category.

THE READER EXHAUSTION EFFECT AND THE ANNUAL REPLACEMENT TARGET

The recognition of the reader exhaustion effect as an important contributory factor to the depreciation of the stock (it will often be found to be the main factor in many non-fiction categories) and, particularly, the discovery of a method of calculating it approximately, reveals that any replacement target based upon it could be extremely wasteful of resources.

In interest categories where the readership is low, the reader exhaustion effect will be high. To cite an example previously given, in the non-fiction category child psychology, the following depreciation rates apply:

Issue life	22 years
Reader exhaustion	5 years
Pre-determined obsolescent rate	12 years

The life of this stock in terms of the issues it will bear is about 22 years. But, the number of continual readers in the category in relation to the desired stock is such that each reader could, theoretically, read all the books in 5 years. According to our rule for assessing the annual replacement rate, the stock would be completely renewed every 5 years. If this were done, a large proportion of the existing stock would be in good physical condition and would also be, to so some extent, currently useful at the end of the period of 5 years. The readers having read what they want will no longer have a use for them. In some interest categories the annual replacement rate on this basis can be as low as one year.

How is the difficulty to be overcome? There are only two possibilities. An independent library must be large enough to ensure that the number of readers it is likely to attract to its smallest interest categories

4

will produce reader exhaustion rates in these categories approximating to the issue life or obsolescence rate for the same categories. The alternative is the exchange of stocks between libraries.

Within a library system having a number of libraries, stocks in interest categories bearing short periods of annual replacement need to be integrated and to be treated as one stock from which readers in all constituent libraries have the opportunity to choose. It will be found, that with the possible exceptions of fiction and biography, many library stocks in urban areas fall to be treated in this way.

Regular exchanges of the stocks in a circuit round the libraries concerned is involved. For purposes of annual purchases of stock, the assessment of the depreciation rates, and hence the appropriate replacement rate, is based on the combined stocks of the interest category in the circuit. The reader exhaustion rates for each of the constituent stocks of a circuit are used then only to indicate the periods over which the exchanges of stock need to take place.

An actual example will better clarify the effects I have referred to. In a series of five branch service points, the interest category child psychology had reader exhaustion rates varying from 6 months to 3 years. If the annual replacements for each of these service points had been treated independently, about 65 new books would be needed to replenish their stocks so as to avoid their exhaustion by the readers. By treating the separate stocks as one unit, the reader exhaustion rate rose to 9½ years for the stock as a whole and needed only 14 books annually for replacement. But, for periods varying between 6 months and 3 years, the combined stock would have to be moved so that the stocks already exhausted by the readers could be replaced by fresh stocks from within the circuit.

THE ANNUAL BOOK TARGET

I have previously indicated a method of calculating the desired stock for each of the interest categories represented in the total circulating stock of the library.

An illustration will remind you of the method:

An interest category, ethics, had 9 books on loan in the highest count of the year. The square root of 9 is 3. The total of all square roots for the library was 1190. The shelf capacity of the library was 17,000 volumes.

The fraction we require, then is $\dfrac{3}{1190} \times 17,000$ which is approximately 43, to which we add the original number on loan, *ie* 9, making 52 as the *desired stock for the category*.

Desired additions for replacements for the ensuing year:

As we have previously shown, the stock is subject to a falling away in the form of various types of depreciation. In order to maintain the desired stock at the level currently assessed, it is necessary to allow for its continuous replacement. An annual estimate of the number of books needed to effect this replacement can be made by taking the figure previously calculated for the desirable stock and dividing this by the period of depreciation appropriate to the interest category. The product represents a theoretical target based on the use of the stock in the interest category at the time that the estimate is made.

Modification of the theoretical target:

In any period prior to the assessment of the current annual target of replacements, the actual level of replacements made could have been inadequate, or even excessive, for a variety of reasons. Annual purchases of fresh stock may have been too low, or there may have been a sudden rise in the readership which would need a rather higher level of stock than could have been justified in previous years.

It may be necessary to modify the theoretical target to take account of past inadequacies in replenishment of stock so that future accession action will be directed towards their correction.

The objects of regular annual accession of additions are:

a) to replace completely the stock over its period of depreciation;

b) to enable the stock to be continuously revised;

c) to ensure that the stock attains a degree of freshness acceptable to the readership.

To enable these objects to be progressively attained, the basis of any modification to the current theoretical target must be sought in the action which has been taken over an immediate past period. A record of the number of purchases and additions in each interest category will provide such a basis. In this way, any falling short which has occurred in the actual replacement rate in the past can be progressively corrected by varying the current theoretical target.

Records for the previous five years in the case of non-fiction and three years in the case of fiction and children's categories will prove satisfactory. If we subtract the annual average of accessions over the appropriate period from the theoretical target figure, we obtain the amount of the discrepancy or modification needed. Adding the modification to the theoretical target produces the Modified target.

For example:

If in an interest category, 400 volumes were purchased over the previous 5 years, the average for each year will be 80. If the current theoretical target is 100, deducting 80 produces a deficiency of 20 which, when added to the theoretical target, produces 120 volumes as the modified target. All other things being equal, the addition of 20 volumes to the target will, over the next five years, correct the error of the previous five years.

It will be realised, of course, that overpurchasing could have taken place in the previous period, resulting in an apparent reduction in the current target figure. In such a case we ignore the modification and retain the theoretical target for the ensuing year, the reason being that however many books may have been purchased in previous years, a continuous flow of new current material is needed by the readership. Over-buying in previous years should not be regarded as a good reason for depriving readers of fresh current material for periods as long as one or two years. In any case, some important individual titles may be published in the new period which, if not purchased, could upset the bibliographical balance of the stock. Any such over-purchasing will need to be dealt with, but it is more appropriately taken care of in the process of revision of stock, to which I refer below.

THE ANNUAL BOOK FUND

Having settled a replacement target for all the interest categories, with modifications where necessary, we have a basis for the determination of the requirements of the annual book fund. Using average costs of purchasing for broad classes of the stock for the immediate previous year we can estimate the cost of purchase for each interest category target, and by combining them obtain a fair estimate of the basic book fund requirements for the ensuing year. To this basic estimate we need to add provision for the bibliographical tools of the trade, reference material and for special revision of interest categories which, for a variety of reasons, call for more drastic revision than the normal annual replacement targets will permit.

The first purpose of a logistical scheme for controlling the book stock has been dealt with, and consists in forming a frame of reference within which the librarian endeavours to build up the stock. The second and no less important purpose is to provide indicators which will enable the librarian to be aware of and to deal with all the factors which may be at work to cause the stock to depreciate, or to depart from the frame of reference which controls its pattern and condition. Whereas the first is achieved by the process of adding to stock, the second is achieved by the process of revising it. The two processes are interlocking and must proceed concurrently, otherwise the process of adding to stock will be rendered to a greater or lesser extent ineffective.

The annual replacement of stock, the assessment of which has been explained, will allow for the addition of newly published material and the replacement of older stock by more bibliographically effective material. In fact, the withdrawal or addition of any title, with the single exception of the replacement of a title by a new copy of the same title, will affect the bibliographical balance of the stock and will thus contain an element of revision. In considering the withdrawal or the addition of any title, therefore, the librarian must take into account its revision effect on the stock of the appropriate interest category. The annual replacement will also allow for the variation from year to year of the distribution of interests within the readership. But the effects of the annual replacement are spread over periods of from three to five years, and there will be circumstances affecting the stock which will suggest that more drastic revision is needed in some interest categories in shorter periods than these.

Over previous periods certain interest categories may have received inadequate attention, inadequate replacements, or may have been affected by changes in readership of an abnormal character. It is also possible that weeding of stock has been erratic as between one category and another, or that some will have received an excessive volume of fresh stocks in relation to others. For all these reasons some interest categories will call for more drastic revision than the annual replacement will permit.

The factors at work within the stock which cause it to depreciate have already been described. Not only will the stock depreciate, but, for the variety of reasons, mainly cumulative in character, just referred to, the stock will depart from the logistical pattern set for it, or else the logistical pattern itself will change. It will do so mainly in two ways:

either the actual stock will exceed the desired stock and thus reduce the available shelf capacity for fresh stock; or the actual stock will fall short of the desired stock and thus reduce the range of choice available to the readers.

Clearly, the conditions which call for revision of stock will vary from one interest category of the stock to the other. We need to know, therefore, what are the distinctive conditions of stock which call for revision, the incidence of these within each interest category, and in which interest category the need for revision is most urgent.

The information we have already acquired about the bookstock will enable us both to identify the conditions calling for revision, and to construct indicators which will show their relative measure and incidence between the various interest categories.

Conditions of stock which will call for revision:

The major conditions and their appropriate indicators are identified and described as follows:

depreciation factors	indicator
1 Proportion of old books is excessive	'age index'.
2 High level of reader exhaustion	'exhaustion level index'.
3 High level of obsolescence	Potentially indicated by the age & exhaustion level indices.
excess and deficiency factors	
4 In excess of desired stock	'excess stock index' and the actual recorded excess.
5 Below desired stock level	'deficiency index' and the actual recorded deficiency.

The indicators: The indicators referred to may be developed as subsequently to be explained.

Age index: An age index of the stock, which will indicate relative urgencies for weeding of stock as between interest categories and libraries within a system, may be obtained by deducting from the figure of actual stock the total purchases over the previous five years, and expressing the balance as a percentage of the actual stock; *eg*, if the actual stock was 1200 volumes and the purchases over the previous 5 years amounted to 300 volumes, then 1200 minus 300 equals 900 which is 75 percent of the actual stock. In this case we know that 75 percent of that stock is over five years old.

The age index may be seen as an indication of the relative freshness or age of the actual stock. It serves especially to correct the reaction that where replacement or purchasing has been considerably below the desirable level, the solution is simply to add more books to bring the actual stock up to the desired level. Clearly, if replacement has been at too low a rate, the actual stock will contain a higher proportion of older books than it should, so that the first step in these circumstances is to 'weed' out the older and less used books. This is essential, although it will further reduce the actual stock as against the desired stock. It will be noted that the 'weeding' action will show up the need for a greater number of fresh additions than would be the case if the first solution is adopted.

Exhaustion level index: As explained in the section on depreciation, the exhaustion of a stock by its readers is likely to be a considerable depreciation factor in interest categories where the loan component is small, although it is operative in all interest categories. The annual replacement rate for the stock of an interest category is arrived at by dividing the estimated desired stock by the appropriate depreciation factor. It will be recalled that the depreciation factors identified were, the *issue life rate*, reflecting the physical life of the stock; the *obsolescence rate*, reflecting the bibliographical condition of the stock; and the reader *exhaustion rate*, reflecting the degree of exhaustion of the stock by the readers. In selecting the factor to be used in calculating the annual replacement, the one calling for the shortest renewal period was to be used. Consequently, whichever depreciation factor is used to determine the annual target for the interest category, it will have taken into account the reader exhaustion rate for the stock. Thus the annual replacement rate will not have been determined by a period of depreciation longer than the reader exhaustion rate itself would have called for. Provided then that the regular addition of fresh stock is maintained at or above the annual replacement rate, the exhaustion of the stock by its readers can be minimised (assuming of course that suitable material has been added).

An indicator which will show whether the reader exhaustion of the stock is being adequately countered is one which reflects the adequacy of the annual replacement rate, or target. In explaining the development of an annual target of additions to stock I also drew attention to the possible need to modify the ideal or theoretical target to take into account deficiencies in replacement action over previous periods of up to five years. I illustrated this point by an example which I will repeat:

If in an interest category, 400 volumes were added over the previous 5 years, the average for each year would have been 80 volumes. If the current theoretical annual target is 100 volumes, then deducting 80 produces a deficiency over the previous period of 20 volumes per annum. Expressed as a percentage of the current theoretical annual target we may say there has been a 20 percent deficiency in past additions or replacements to the stock, or we may say that the theoretical annual target has to be increased by 20 percent to make up for past deficiencies.

This correction factor for the annual target, if plotted on a percentage scale of 100, indicates the degree to which the addition of fresh stock to the interest category has exceeded or fallen short of the annual target. If the factor is positive it will indicate a degree of under-replacement and will, therefore, also indicate the extent to which 'reader exhaustion' may be affecting the particular stock. Used on a percentage scale I describe it as the exhaustion level index.

Obsolescence indicator: The bibliographical condition of the stock cannot be expressed in numerical terms, but the age index and the exhaustion level index will, if taken together, form a valuable potential indication. If both indices are of a relatively high order then we can safely assume that the bibliographical condition of the stock is in urgent need of attention.

Excess stock indicator: When the actual stock exceeds the desired stock it is simple to express the difference as a percentage of the desired stock. For example, if the desired stock is assessed to be 200 volumes and the actual stock is 250 volumes, then the excess may be expressed as $\frac{50}{200}$ which equals 25 percent. The actual number of volumes in excess can be shown on a book selector's record, and in percentage form it will be possible to relate it to comparable figures in other interest categories.

Deficiency indicator: It will be obvious that the actual stock may be below the assessed desired stock. This difference, a negative one, can also be expressed as a percentage of the desired stock. For example, if the desired stock is assessed at 200 volumes and the actual stock is 150 volumes, then there is a deficiency of 50 volumes, or 25 percent. In these circumstances, a degree of replenishment or building up of stock is indicated.

Replenishment, *ie* bringing the stock up to the level of the desired stock, is as important as weeding. For although the annual target, as modified, may correct for partial under-purchasing, it does so over a long period. If there is a considerable discrepancy between actual and desired stock, a modified annual target may take too long to correct the position. Even should the actual stock be composed of recent and suitable books (following, for example, a substantial weeding out of old and obsolete books), it offers too few books to choose from. The readership is likely to decline, and if the position is not corrected relatively quickly, the annual target is itself likely to decline. An index of urgency for replenishment is as necessary, therefore, as an index for weeding.

Urgency for revision:

The indicators just explained which suggest the need for revision may be summarised as follows:

a) Age index

b) Exhaustion level index

c) Excess stock index

d) Replenishment index.

Should any one of these indicators be abnormally high, the condition of the particular stock needs urgent attention. The relative urgency of revision as between one interest category and another may be assessed by taking the highest rating shown by any one of the indicators relating to the category, and comparing it with the highest rating of any one of the indicators for other interest categories. As each kind of indicator is a measure of the need for some condition of the stock calling for revision, the question of urgency is not affected by comparing say, an age index of one category with an excess stock value for another category.

It should be noted that these indicators reflect the respective conditions as they affect the whole of the circulating stock in an interest category, *ie* books both on loan and on the shelves.

It is not possible to demonstrate here the practical effects which such a systematic approach can produce, nor to elaborate on its effects upon the overall library organisation, staff structure, the arrangement of stock and its classification and cataloguing. All these activities need to be integrated. Yet no matter how efficacious the logistical operations may be in setting guidelines for the bibliographical operations, effective book provision is in the last analysis dependent on the latter. A sound logistical system will not correct errors committed in the bibliographical field. It will, however, reveal them more quickly, indicate where they are likely to be having the worst effect on the stock, and possibly point the way to their correction. It will produce a programme of priorities essential to the most effective use of resources, and will, if operated within an appropriate staff structure, release the librarian to concentrate on his bibliographical activities.

APPENDIX I

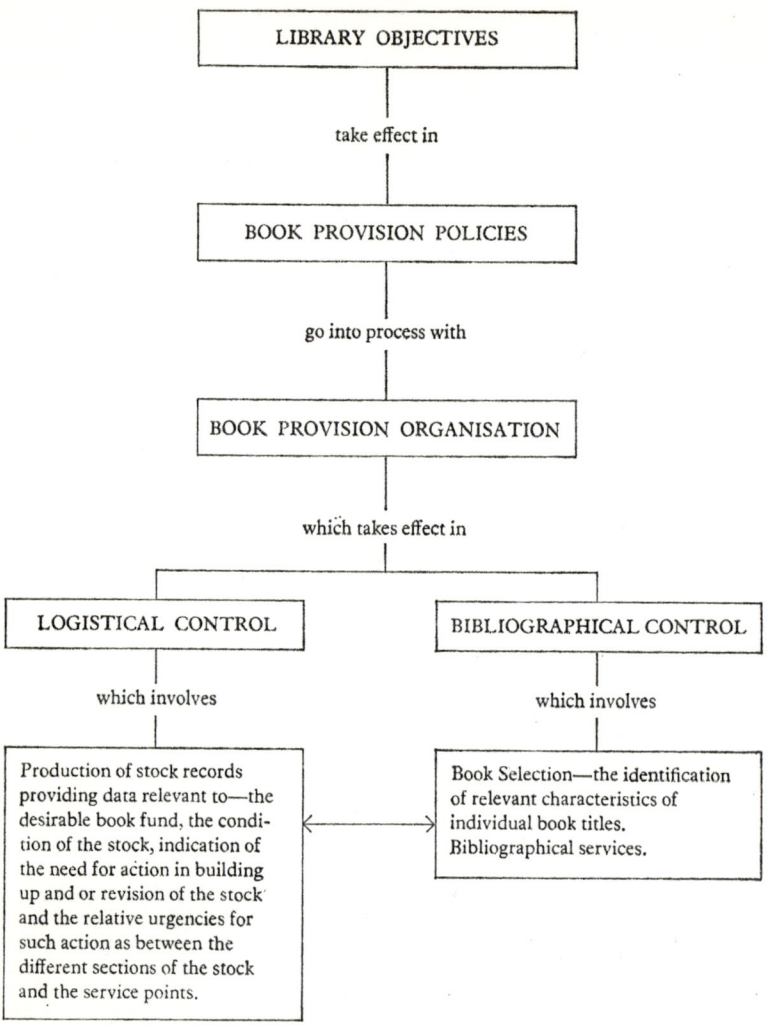

The theory of objectives as the factor in book provision.

SCALE OF ACCESSIBILITY

IMMEDIATE	DEFERRED				NONE

CIRCULATING STOCK

Shelf Stock	On loan to Readers	Out of Circulation (Binding etc.)	Purchasable Items (New or Secondhand)	Subscription Libraries (e.g. Law Notes) etc.)	Other Libraries Inter-Lending	Yet to be Written
'Shelf Component'	'Loan' Component					

DEPENDENT ON DEGREE
OF PHYSICAL ACCESSIBILITY

OTHER
LIBRARIES
IN
SYSTEM

SUSPENSE STOCKS TEMPORARILY WITHDRAWN
RESERVE STOCKS

Scale of accessibility. Diagrammatic form.

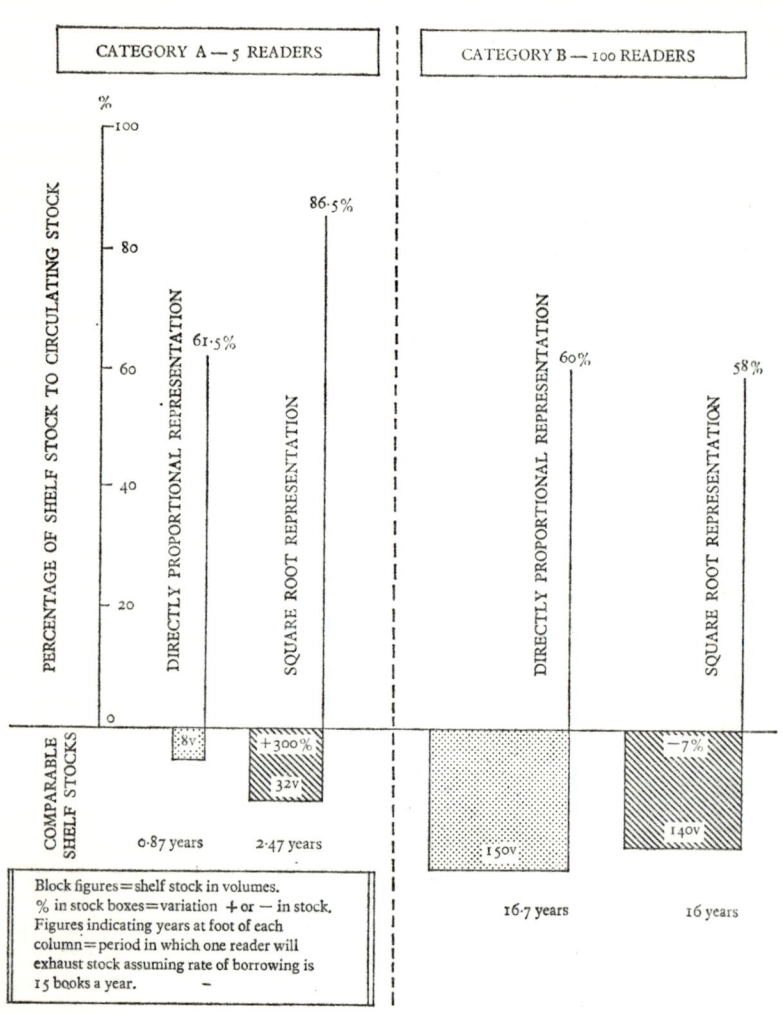

Effects on shelf stock of different methods of representation.

APPENDIX IV

STOCK RECORD CARDS ARRANGED IN VISIBLE INDEX FORM FOR GUIDANCE OF SUBJECT LIBRARIANS CONCERNED WITH BIBLIOGRAPHICAL OPERATIONS.

Eleven cards are shown for Fiction Categories and except for the top card (Fo) bottom edge of each card only is visible at a glance.

The card or cards bearing the highest number in the last righthand section relate to those categories requiring the most urgent attention of the librarian.

Fo

CENTRAL LIBRARY   1965

Interest Category   (Library)   (Year)
(Class Nos.

SPECIAL INSTRUCTIONS

This scale is used when revision or withdrawal of volumes is indicated: provisional withdrawal for title inspection is made by removing from circulation those books showing 'issues' thus ←

MEAN ISSUE PER BOOK SCALE

M	22
3	16½
2	11
1	5½

TARGET			Jan.	Feb.	Mar.	Apr.	May	June	July	Aug.	Sept.	Oct.	Nov.	Dec.	Total		
T 1236	n	PURCHASES TO DATE	42 4)	167 90	195 115	194	485	517	548	587	632	700	719	766	766	Desired Stock (D)	3708
Tm	App.T.	TARGET BALANCE	1312	1263	1238	1159	868	836	805	766	721	649	635	587	587	Actual Stock (A)	2847
																Diff + or-	− 86.

Desired Stock (D) 3708
Actual Stock (A) 2847
Diff + or- − 86.

n 100 / T	(1)	F = (A − P) x 100 / A (2)	3/5 years Purchases (P)	Y = − 'P' converted to + (3)	X = (A − D) x 100 / D (4)	Highest of (1),(2),(3),(4)
			3359			

Allocations and £ Level Index		Age Index (F)		Topping-Up Index (Y)			Excess Index (X)		Rev. Priority Index	
−		− 19					− 18			18
#			FO	18						
+			F1	13						
+			F2.	13½						
+			F3	16						
+			F4	20					20	
+			F5	31					31	
+			F6	3						
+			F7							
+			F8	5						
+			F9	10						
+			CF.	13						

These categories call for relatively urgent attention by additions to stock.

9: *What are we up to?*

IN RECENT YEARS I had gained the impression that our younger librarians were becoming too narrowly professional in their outlook. It seemed to me that they had developed a conservative and even arrogant attitude about the role of the public library. This attitude could be summarised crudely as 'I am a librarian, an expert; I know what is good for you the reader; and I am going to provide you with what you should read; if you don't like what I provide, you can go elsewhere.' The word 'demand', as an expression of what readers wanted to read, took on a somewhat dirty connotation. There appeared to have developed an aversion to the administrative and organisational aspects of the library in favour of a concentration on books for their own sake and a disregard of what books were for.

In the continuous attempt to keep our heads above the ever rising waters of inflation, we were becoming obsessed with the necessity for professional status. The direct linking of salaries with qualification levels accentuated the process. Thus, during a period which has been characterised by an amount of professional educational activity never before experienced, we have been diverted from considering the ends we serve. Instead we have been concerned with the labels to be gained from our education and the work we do. This may be part of the price that society has to pay when it fails to reward some of its members at their proper value. Nevertheless, we can hardly expect society to recognise our proper value if we are not too sure about it ourselves.

Some 12 years ago I wrote a group of articles intended to implant the idea that what we were concerned with mainly was the use and reading of books, and that the reader is as much a part of these activities as are the books. I thought we needed to know as much about the users and readers of books as we do about books. This idea failed to evoke much response. It has taken Mr Raymond Williams and a few others of a similar frame of mind to stir us to a sense of our responsibility towards those we serve and the society which supports us. It was refreshing to see these ideas and the nature of our responsibility expressed in the admirable Library Association prize essay by Frank Hatt and published in the *Library Association record* October 1961. During a recent discussion with students of the North-Western Polytechnic school of librarianship the question was posed 'Are librarians more concerned with the means, rather than the ends of librarianship? '. The question itself revealed a new awareness, and the answers that followed indicated that the social function of the public library and its relation with the culture of society were appreciated as being high among its purposes.

I have been encouraged therefore to offer some thoughts on the theme of the ends we serve, or, in the prosaic terms of my title ' What are we up to? '.

Discussions on a great many professional matters, and in particular on this theme, suffer from a failure to distinguish between the ends of librarianship and the ends of the public library service. Too often it is assumed that they are one and the same. This is incorrect and is a source of great confusion. The public library is one kind of library among a number of different kinds of libraries. There are private libraries, institutional libraries, government libraries, national libraries, industrial and business libraries and public libraries. Each is organised towards its own particular ends. Sociologically speaking they may all serve certain general ends in common, but each will do its best by having a clear understanding of its own particular functions.

The librarian, however, is a professional worker. This means simply that he offers certain services, based on specialised training and skills, to whomsoever can usefully employ them. In this respect he is no different from any other professional workers. He is distinguished merely by the kind of service he can offer. His particular kind of service is described as librarianship. The ends of librarianship therefore are concerned with service and its improvement, through increased skills and the development of improved techniques and methods of organisation. We reach then, the apparently paradoxical position, that the ends of librarianship are the means by which other ends are served.

As there are different kinds of libraries, each with its particular ends, so there will be different kinds of librarian. Each librarian needs to adapt his skills and modify his application of them to suit the ends of the particular library he serves. If he is to do this successfully it is obvious that he will need to be clear about these. For most this situation is understood and perfectly acceptable. The librarian's personal attitude to the ends of the library he serves may range from neutral to one of positive identification. If he found himself greatly at variance with the ends of the library, he would normally try to find another where they were more acceptable. It is difficult to imagine a fervent nuclear-disarmer librarian serving a library whose ends were concerned with the development of nuclear weapons. In any case, it is most unlikely that he would be afforded the opportunity to do so.

The position of the public librarian is somewhat different. He is not clear about the ends his type of library serves. It appears to be much more difficult to determine what they are. In most other kinds of libraries the governing body determines the ends to be served, but in the case of the public library the governing body is no more certain of what they should be than the librarian. Perhaps the only commonly accepted end is that the library exists for the public good but in what that 'good' consists is almost anybody's guess. There's the rub—anybody's guess!

Many public librarians, as a result of years of familiarity with books, with the continuous need to bring order out of chaos, and the acquisition of a habit of service in their work, develop a sense of responsibility, a thoughtful attitude to men and affairs, and ideas of the values of books. In the absence of pre-determined ends for the public library, librarians may be tempted to substitute for them their own personal ends and values. Thus, by an unconscious transposition of roles, the librarian's own ends become the ends of the public library he serves. No matter how noble or responsible his values may be, he thereby commits a grievous error. By making the ends of the library a reflection of his own personal values he renders himself open to challenge from his governing body, from his readers and from society at large. As essentially a servant, he is on weak ground to meet the challenge.

To avoid this temptation it is necessary to keep in mind the distinction made earlier between the ends of librarianship and the ends of the public library service. If the public librarian is not to be permitted to shape the ends of his library service in accordance with his personal values, what then is to be done? The librarian is the most concerned with the problem because, unless it is resolved in such a way that he knows what he is expected to aim for, he cannot apply his specialised skills to create an effective service. He is therefore entitled to seek a solution, but it will need to be one which stems from independently verifiable terms of reference.

What information conforming to these requirements is available?

a) The public library is a particular kind of library.

b) It is a charge on public funds.

c) For all practical purposes its use is not restricted by law to any class or group of people.

d) Its government is subject to a democratic process so that all citizens are in the position to bring pressure to bear on its regulation, conduct, provision and service.

e) The nature of the books available in and through the library is not restricted in any way except as may be determined by the governing body.

f) The need for various forms of co-operation between independently controlled public libraries is recognised and provided for.

g) The size and number of libraries within the control of the governing body is entirely within its discretion.

This information provides the indisputable framework within which the public library service operates. Specifically, the purposes of the service are not referred to, but are they implicit within the information given? I think they are.

We are concerned with the provision of a public library which, being one kind of library, will embody in its ends the purposes which are common to all kinds of libraries. A library is a system of storage and retrieval, a storage of recorded knowledge and experience organised so as to make any part of it available as and when required. But what makes the public library different in kind? The answer given is accessibility. The library must be available to all citizens and, so as to eliminate any possible restriction, it must be available freely. The recognition of the need for co-operation between independently controlled libraries implies further that accessibility is not to be limited to the recorded knowledge and experience stored in the one library or system. It is implied that, potentially, there should be free accessibility to all recorded knowledge and experience. The framework of information makes two value assumptions: that the function of a library and the right of accessibility to it are significant for all members of society, whether as individuals they make use of it or not.

The central significance of accessibility to all recorded knowledge and experience is underlined by the absence of any restriction or guidance as to the nature of the contents of the library.

These then are the legitimate terms of reference within which the public librarian has to work. The ends of librarianship for him may be summarised in the following terms:

a) His function is one of service to a particular community.

b) He has to collect together and maintain a store of books and related material which continuously reflects the book and reading needs of that community, to the extent that these are not otherwise provided for on terms of unrestricted accessibility.

c) Each level and field of interest has an equal right to his services.

d) His permanent and major aim is to organise bibliographical and retrieval services which will obtain for his library users the greatest practicable degree of access to all recorded knowledge and experience.

This is what we are up to.

Is it too uninspiring a prospect? What about the educational function of libraries? What about the function of improving the level of books read? What about the cultural responsibilities of libraries? What about all the other 'do good' functions of libraries? Does it amount only to giving people what they want?

Please don't all rush off with your resignations in hand. The point is that our terms of reference do not permit the ends implied in these questions to be set up as ends for the public library. To do so is simply to confuse the ends of librarianship and the ends of the public library with our own personal ends and values. Is there no inspiration in the ends I have posed? A closer examination of their implications, especially viewed within the social situation in which we operate, will surely show that there is.

I would commend the reading of *Learning, remembering and knowing* by Patrick Meredith, Professor of Psychology at the University of Leeds. The place of the library in the system of organised knowledge, and the significance of books and reading for the individual are simply and splendidly outlined: ' If you have stood on a roof during an air-raid and watched a large public library blazing and, amidst all the other distractions, felt the peculiar wantonness of this particular set-back to man's civilising impulse, you will begin to ponder on the strange power which is the daily business of these quiet functionaries . . . We are getting used to the idea that in the new nuclear power stations the consumption of one nuclear fuel may not only produce power for immediate use but also breed a second type of fuel. The library is an even more remarkable transformer of energy for the " fuel " which goes into it, in the form of books and journals, not only gives out a steady flow of power through all its readers, many of whom produce further books themselves; it remains itself intact, preserving its energy undiminished. This is the unique property of organised and recorded knowledge . . . Words, words, words, flowing out from the library, into countless minds, opening them to new actions, new experiences, new powers, new worlds. And these catalysts of brain-action, having done their work, return to the library unchanged, ready to do it again as often as needed. And as a result homes are made more attractive, careers are made more effective, committees are made more productive, time is more meaningfully spent, the oceans and generations are bridged, and the mind of civilisation, triumphing over space, time and matter, becomes ever more articulate and purposive. This is the power-transformation in which you are participating every time you open a book.'

This surely is inspiration enough to work in any kind of library? But the public library's purpose is to guarantee the unrestricted access of all citizens, not only to one biblio-powerhouse but to the whole biblio-power system. Words, words, words are flowing not only from the library into countless minds, but from many other systems of communication as well. With the exception of libraries it is characteristic of almost all systems of communication today that words are flowing which are designed to control, to shape and to mould countless minds. If these are not the deliberate objects of certain power groups, then the system of communication can only be maintained if it persists in policies of accepted and established modes of thought and feeling. The supreme danger for civilisation and the individual lies not only in the possibility of the atomic explosion, for, as James Thurber has foreseen, one girl, one boy and one flower are likely to survive. An equal danger lies in the persistence of patterns of communication which restrict the flow of minority modes of thought and feeling. The effect of this is to prevent the mind of civilisation adjusting its schemas or perceptions in time to cope with the revolutionary changes in the human environment. This state of affairs justifies James Thurber's further prediction that the one girl, the one boy and the one flower will restart the whole process which will once again end in the devastation of this earth. Were not our victorian forefathers acutely wise, or perhaps, wiser than they knew, when they saw the central purpose of the public library as the guaranteeing of completely free and unrestricted access for every citizen to the whole of recorded knowledge and experience?

The public library is the one line of communication which seeks neither to exploit, control or mould. Professor Meredith accurately pinpoints the contrast between the purposes of education and of reading. He says: ' The child on entering school enters on a life of organisation . . . The timetable organises his activities. The materials, pictures, books and other apparatus organise his stream of perceptions. The teacher and the other children organise his attitudes and his social consciousness. The pattern and rhythm of all this organisation go on throughout his educational career. The curriculum and the examinations organise his intellectual processes. Unfortunately the better the organisation the less well equipped he is, on leaving school, to undertake the organisation of his own life.' He goes on, 'For reading is a process of self-discovery as well as a pathway to knowledge. The adolescent cannot escape reorganisation . . . Books are the gentlest and most accommodating of reorganisers. The reader can reorganise his mind at his own pace and on his own terms.' The public library affords the opportunity to the individual to engage in the process of self-discovery and to *reorganise himself*. By keeping open this freely accessible line of communication, the public library ensures that all modes of thought and feeling, all ideas, no matter how slightly represented in society, have an audience, an opportunity of expression and assimilation, if viable. Is this central purpose not an inspiration for service?

Then there is the question of the 'cultural gap'. Raymond Williams, Joseph Trenamen and others have drawn attention to the dangerous situation in which a cultural curtain is growing up within our society. A new class alignment is appearing; on the one hand a cultured educated class and on the other, the mass-pressure anti-culture class, with the latter increasingly in a position to exert pressure on the instruments of power. This again reflects the communication pattern. Too many people are attempting to control and exploit, to tell others what they should do and what they should think. Precisely because the public library is the one system of communication whose central purpose is not to make such attempts, it has the best opportunity for eliminating the cultural curtain. If we substitute our personal ends for the public library ends we should fail completely in using such an opportunity. We must accept that the basis of all self-discovery and paths to knowledge is through interest, an interest in something. One of the positive gains from the spread of radio and television has been its power of stimulating interests among wide numbers of people. The public library must provide opportunity for all interests to be developed and satisfied. We must overcome the notion that what is good for us is good for others, and not be afraid to provide for all levels of interest, so that whatever the interest and at whatever level it starts, we do not kill it by restrictions based on an insatiable desire to do good. Any other attitude will positively accentuate the extension of the 'cultural curtain'.

The ends of public librarianship, then, serve the library as a biblio-powerhouse, a technical invention as significant for humanity as any other; they ensure universal accessibility to all recorded knowledge and experience, thus preserving them against the effects of conformism and exploitation; and they accept responsibility for ensuring a classless society in the cultural sense. Is there not inspiration and stimulation for creative thinking enough in these? I think there is. Are they not worthy enough that we have to find other ends? I think they are, and that we do not need to seek other ends.

We have said that the ends of librarianship were the means to the ends which we have tried to elucidate. The crux of the problem for us as practising librarians is the means. How do the ends which have been set affect us in this respect?

I think we may say that the problem is focused on two major activities; the organisation of book provision, and the organisation of bibliographical and retrieval services. It may be argued that all that has been said so far amounts to no more than licence to organise book collections simply in accordance with what people want. That would be a superficial argument and an indication that my theme has been misunderstood. Even if that were the object it would not be possible, if only because the resources and accommodation of the library are limited. It would be possible, of course, to allow the collection to be built up strictly in accordance with the demands made for books. Within the limited accommodation available this would entail many people remaining unsatisfied. But more unfortunate, it would lead directly into a collection based on the tyranny of the majority, which runs completely counter to our overall objectives. It will be noted that I have used the expression ' book provision ' in preference to ' book selection '. I do so because our objectives demand a relationship with the reader of ' provision ' as against ' selection ' or restriction. This is significant because, although we have to observe principles of economy which compel us to select or filter, we are obliged to accept that our library is not an island and our bibliographical organisation will be geared to ' provision ' regardless of whether what is needed is immediately available or not. The concept of provision also permits the selection or filter policy to take into account the fact that the library collection is not the limit of recorded knowledge and experience for its readers. Although the idea of provision has seeped into our professional practice, as for example through forms of co-operation, nevertheless the tradition of seeing our library collection as an island still exercises a considerable influence on book selection policies.

The prime impulse to reading is interest, an interest in something specific, or a broader general interest. It would seem logical therefore to make our stock reflect the interests among our readers. Let it be said here that interest and demand are not synonymous. Demand does not take into account the needs of the reader who is not aware of specific books or even of specific subjects. This will be frequently the case during the process of individual self-discovery. If our stock is built up on 'interest units' it is possible to cater for the unexpressed interest or demand. As we cannot evaluate interests in the sense of whether or not one is better than another, we must treat them all as being equally entitled to representation.

We have made the point that the library is not an island. Within the limited resources of one library we can only take limited measures to ensure accessibility to books for minority interests. For some of these interests it will not be possible to have enough books continuously available to ensure that all the potentially interested readers have been attracted to make use of them. The range of choice will inevitably be too small. We must develop methods which will for adequate periods provide a fully adequate range of choice in these cases. Within one library system comprising a number of libraries the difficulty can be met partially by bringing together the books from each library falling into one 'interest unit' and shelving them at each library in turn. But even this will not be sufficient in all cases. In our subject specialisation schemes we have the making of another possibility. In a subject specialising library or among a group of libraries within a region, there will be collections of books offering a wide range of choice in a minority interest field, and which by being split up or located in one library only are little used. Could we not organise from such sources substantial loan collections for deposit over adequate periods in various libraries in turn? By this means we might test the degree of interest present among our own readership.

I have referred to the reader with a specific interest whose requirements cannot be met immediately. No matter how carefully 'interest units' are built up there will be many instances where a specific title has to be located and obtained from outside the library. The accessibility of the stock in such instances is measured by the reader in terms of the time it takes to get the book to him. We need to reduce this time factor to the minimum. This again calls for the closer integration of the independent library systems. The importance of accessibility in this sense I have dealt with in another paper (see chapter 7), but I mention it here to complete the picture of the ends deriving from the framework of information we have about the public library.

As it seems to me, there need be little confusion about our purposes. I think it is clear however, that to achieve them we need to dispense with some traditional attitudes. Our attitude needs to be reader-centred rather than book-centred. I think I cannot conclude better than by again quoting Professor Meredith: 'We have heard a lot in recent years about the relation of men to machines. We have given too little thought to the relation of men to books.'

10: *A systems approach to libraries*

WHAT do we mean by Systems Approach?

We mean the application of the technique, usually referred to as systems analysis, to an organisation and its constituent operations. Current interest in systems analysis is almost certainly due to the impact of computers on so many spheres of activity. In a computer application it becomes essential to break down an operation into its simplest elemental steps, the omission of any one of which may not only nullify the effectiveness of the operation, but render the computer output useless.

However, the use of systems analysis is not exclusively related to computer applications. As a concept systems analysis is but a sophisticated form of what good administrators (currently termed ' managers ') have employed long before the term became current. By system is meant any co-ordinated organisation of things, processes or activities arranged to achieve certain ends. Systems analysis proceeds by probing an existing system, identifying its essential features and reconstructing the system or creating a new one which will meet the requirements or objectives of the system in the simplest or most efficient way *Simplification is the keynote of the outcome*, '. . . a new system ought to be a simplification of the old as the trappings of years of operation and amendment are cleared away '.[1] We must not confuse simplification with a system of few parts; in nature the more highly developed and significant systems become more complex and consist of many parts, each of which has evolved to operate in the simplest and most effective way. To simplify by reducing the number of parts or steps within a system is, as likely as not, to render the system redundant and ineffective.

We can consider the pattern of an organisation as a system to be analysed, or we can consider the *complex of operations* which enable the organisation to function, individually as distinct systems to be analysed. Whichever of these we choose to consider, we must investigate not only the particular organisation or operation but the *environment* within which it operates. For example, an analysis of an operation in *isolation* may suggest a simpler, more efficient or more economic way of doing it, but if the new method produces a lessening of efficiency, a greater complexity or an increased workload *elsewhere* within the organisation, or, if it involves some measure of sacrifice of the overall objectives which it is designed to achieve, then the outcome of the analysis is not the desirable one.

We should recognise, therefore, that there are important conditions attaching to the systems approach, they are :

a) That the *context* within which a system operates must be investigated as well as the system itself, and from which it follows that we must avoid 'putting the cart before the horse', by probing and designing the overall organisation of which individual systems form a part, before dealing with the latter.

b) That the definition of *objectives* must be clarified, both of the organisation and its parts, so that the new or reconstructed systems are designed to meet their proper requirements.

Applied to the library field this means that the library as a *total system*, and the *social context* within which it operates, must first be analysed, and in the light of the analysis an appropriately designed system developed. Essential, therefore, to the exercise will be the clarification and definition of the library system's objectives, so that in analysing its constituent systems these will be designed to contribute effectively to the achievement of those objectives.

The value of a clarification and a statement of objectives as a primary requisite lies in the fact that it provides a criterion for deciding :

a) What operations fail to contribute to the objectives.

b) What kinds of processes will be better able to meet objectives.

c) How we can ensure that the improved processes are meeting the objectives.

Of course it will be argued that it is difficult to be very precise about library objectives, especially in the case of the public library. However, this very difficulty reinforces the need to try to achieve greater precision. The vaguer the definition of objectives, the more precariously balanced will be the whole edifice of organisation and processes which constitute the library services, and the more readily will it totter in the varying directions of the fashionable and the superficial, its potentialities underestimated, its significance attacked, and its future control placed at the mercy of alien interests. Our principal theme, therefore, is not to describe and explain the more sophisticated techniques of systems analysis; there are many better able to do this; nor, to provide a series of examples of its application to libraries, but to emphasise the primacy of objectives for libraries and the value of a systems approach, both to the identification and clarification of these objectives, and the design of the plan and organisation required to meet them.

How do we set about defining the library's objectives? One method could be to ask a number of librarians, and possibly others concerned with the government of libraries, what they consider to be the objectives; to co-relate the answers and formulate a concensus of opinion from them. Or the historical record could be examined with a view to ascertaining the motivations for establishing libraries in the first place. Either method, the pragmatic or the historic, is likely to result in a definition somewhat subjective in character, and open to modifications as attitudes and social climates change. A less subjective approach which is more consonant with the underlying principles of the systems approach is needed, that is, a systematic method.

The systematic method would be concerned to establish first, the possibilities of the library as a general type of organisation, the environment or context within which it operates, and how the library's possibilities are modified thereby. It would then consider which of its particular inherent possibilities as a general type need to be *emphasised* in a particular type or class of the library species. From these considerations a set of objectives would be derived.

The analysis can then be extended through a series of questions and answers:

What is the nature of the library as an organisation? Essentially it is a storage and retrieval mechanism.

What does it store and retrieve? Books. (This answer may be true only in a very limited sense. The book itself is only a device; it may be that what is ultimately the subject of storage and retrieval is what the book can offer or provide.)

What is the context within which it operates? It is a social invention forming part of the *total system of communication* which in turn is vital to the functioning of society.

What are the features of the *book process* of communication which distinguish it from other processes of communication and which give it its particular significance?

What are the features of the library which distinguish it from other organisations for communication concerned with the distribution of books?

From the answers to those questions we could derive a definition of the purpose and potentialities of *libraries in general*. But to define the

118

objectives of a *particular type of library* we need to ask, 'What is the nature of the authority which supports the library?,' for this will determine its type or class and its specific potentialities.

The objectives, having been defined, will form the criteria for the validity and utility of all the elements in the *designed organisation*. The principal element in the design is the principal function of the library, that is to say, *book provision*. Before any other element can be considered we must decide the policies of book provision to be pursued. These will be conditioned by:

The objectives of the library.

The potential clientele.

The relationships of the library with other sources for books.

The process by which book provision policies are to be achieved is in the nature of a *storage and retrieval mechanism,* the elements of which comprise:

The storage system.

The users or readers.

The retrieval organisation.

The factors affecting storage are:

Supply of material and relationships with other stores.

Form taken by the store—static, *ie* non-circulating; fluid, *ie* circulating; unitary, *ie* one store only; or serial *ie* a series of connected stores.

Capacity of storage system.

Demands upon the store, involving nature and composition of the clientele, range of acceptable demands.

The retrieval organisation.

The factors affecting users or readers are:

Range of acceptable readership.

Motivations of readership, *ie* the kinds of uses to be expected; the potential interests within the readership.

Nature of storage and retrieval systems, particularly as they affect the levels of accessibility to them afforded to the readership.

The factors affecting retrieval are:

Behaviour patterns of clientele.

Form taken by the store.

From these elements we can construct a development chart for designing the organisation, which will indicate the order and nature of the *data* and *decisions* needed. Figure 6 illustrates in a simplified form how such a chart might look. The upper half of the chart indicates both the range of data and the areas in which decisions are required. On the basis of the information forthcoming from these, the design of the organisation can be developed.

LIBRARY OBJECTIVES
take effect in
|
BOOK PROVISION POLICIES
which go into process
with
|
BOOK PROVISION ORGANISATION
which takes account
of
|

READERSHIP	ACCESSIBILITY RETRIEVAL SYSTEMS	BOOKSTOCK
Behaviour	*Stores and sub-stores*	*Acquisition*
motivations	Arrangement of library	Systematic development
use	Shelf arrangement	Systematic maintenance
interests	Internal stores	Regulation
	External stores	
	Locations system	
	Bibliographical services	

produces
|
ORGANISATION PLANS
|

Administrative and
Operational plan══════════*Staff plan*══════════*financial plans*

Operational plan	*Staff plan*	*Administrative and financial plans*
Systems and methods	Bibliographical and technical	Administrative services
Feedback systems	Locations and distributive	Budgetary controls
	Administrative and financial	

FIGURE 6

The *organisation plan* will require the creation of a number of operational systems and methods, which together will achieve the integrated implementation of the library objectives within the resources available. It is in the working out of these systems and methods that the application of the techniques of *systems analysis* can be most valuable. The organisation plan will determine the particular objectives of each operation. These objectives may be regarded as *secondary* or *sub-objectives,* as distinct from the *primary objectives* of the library. The organisation plan must ensure that the *secondary objectives* of all the operations are both necessary to and in conformity with the *primary objectives.* An example of the appropriateness of this distinction between primary and secondary objectives is afforded by the frequently occurring problem in public libraries of the excessive reservation of books by readers. The problem can arise from a rate of reservations which, either in total or in the case of one title, appears to be such that staff cannot cope with it, or else the required duplication of titles is more than existing resources will permit. If the problem is viewed in isolation, that is to say without regard to the primary objectives of the library, then it might be solved by some restriction on the acceptability of reservations, or by increasing the fee for reservations so as effectively to price them down to an acceptable level. If, however, the problem is viewed in relation to the primary objectives, the solution might take a very different form; one which, perhaps, does not restrict the number of reservations, but introduces an improved administrative system for dealing with them, coupled possibly with a scale of priorities which readers could be induced to accept as reasonable and fair.

Systems analysis will indicate the appropriate kinds of data needed to make the operation possible, and will, by the use of mathematical and related techniques, evolve the simplest and most effective method of carrying out the operation. Systems analysis will also show what operations or parts of operations are likely to be suitable for computer application.

Already systems analysis has been applied to a number of operations and problems in the library field, among which may be cited for example:

Circulation problems; such as the estimating of demand; the effects of reducing loan periods for some categories of books—work in this direction has produced data which could improve accessibility to the bookstock—it would involve introducing varying loan periods for different sections of the stock according to the ways in which they are used; this is not an entirely new practice, because commonsense or expediency has dictated such a practice in limited circumstances; nevertheless, the practice could be extended considerably with benefit to readers and the better exploitation of the bookstocks; the effects of duplicating titles and the vexing problems associated with reservations, already referred to, have been studied.

Stock control; A more sophisticated control or regulation of bookstocks may be possible with the aid of these techniques. It could be possible to keep a close watch on the condition of the stock in all its sections, pinpointing those calling for urgent attention, indicating approximately the nature of their deficiencies; calculating a realistic book fund based on the actual state of the stock within a particular period.

These are a few of the possibilities in what may be regarded as the principal area of the library's operations. Other areas are *readers' registration* (why do we want this?), and *accessions registration*.

It may be significant that the pioneering work in the application of systems analysis to libraries has been done in association with university libraries both in the UK and the USA. The reasons for neglect in this respect so far as public libraries are concerned may be:

a) Librarians in university libraries are in closer touch with the experts in systems analysis and its association with the computer.

b) Systems analysis utilises mathematical techniques at a level of sophistication not commonly to be found among public librarians or those with whom they are normally associated. The public library probably attracts those who are less numerate in outlook and who often tend to be ' do-it-yourselfers '. First attempts at trying to understand the techniques involved can be baffling and the ' do-it-yourselfer ' feels that it isn't for him.

c) The primary objectives of the non-public library are likely to be more concrete and precise than they are for the public library.

The essential preliminary for the public library, if its operations are to benefit from the use of systems analysis, is a systems approach to its primary objectives, so that these can be clarified and made more precise. Otherwise, the organisation plan of the library will not ensure that all parts of the organisation are making an effective contribution to the service. The very looseness of the objectives may result in various parts pressing forward at different rates and in different directions. similarly, the secondary objectives of the various operations will not be adequately conditioned by the primary objectives, and the application of systems analysis to any of them may result in an actual weakening or diminution of the service available to the users. For example, the computerisation of the catalogue, because it has to adapt to the limitations of the computer, may lead to a loss of information reducing its ultimate value to the user. Further, the application of operations piecemeal to the computer may well involve much additional and wasteful work as each operation is processed independently. Ideally, it is necessary to consider the whole system of operations in relation to the computer.

In considering the application of systems analysis to the public library we do not need to enhance establishments with posts for systems analysts. Many of the operations which lend themselves to systems analysis are common to all public libraries. What we need are models which we can use, but these models need to be translated into the form of *administrative* procedures which can be applied readily by the non-numerate. Those librarians in the universities who have been associated with the pioneer work could perform a valuable service if, in collaboration with public librarians, they would assist in working out just such procedures. However, before much progress can be made in this direction the public library needs more adequate data, especially in the areas of readership behaviour in relation to books and the library apparatus—readers are the subject of the library's activity, yet the least studied field—and, the environment and context within which the public library operates—its relationships and significance in the overall communication system.

REFERENCE

1 Robinson, Clough and others: *Systems analysis in libraries.* Oriel Press, 1969.

See also

Buckland, Hindle and others: *Systems analysis of a university library: final report on a research project.* University of Lancaster Occasional Papers no 4. University of Lancaster Library, 1970.

Morse, Philip M: *Library effectiveness: a systems approach.* Cambridge, Massachusetts, MIT Press, 1968.

11: *The purpose of libraries*

WE MAY question the need to even consider the purpose of libraries. Anyone who uses a library will assume that its purpose is to acquire a stock of books and to make them available to those people who want them. To understand purpose in this sense is to mistake purpose for function, to describe the library as an instrument and its fundamental principle of operation. It does not tell us why such an instrument should be used, how it should be used, or what ends it should serve.

It has been said that institutions are the mechanisms of society and as such are not good in themselves but only in the service of life.[1] In other words, institutions, of which the library is one, are as good as the human ends which they serve.

So, in talking of purpose we are talking of the human ends which the library, as a social instrument, should sustain and pursue. Without an understanding of the ends served by his library the librarian possesses no consistent criteria by which he can assess the value or utility of his actions. He does not know what books his library should acquire, nor what groups of readers are to be accepted as its users.

Consideration of purpose for the library is, more often than not, concerned with deriving criteria for the acquisition and maintenance of book stocks. Important as this may be, it is hardly less important for guidance in the determination of the way in which the library is to be organised, the kinds of staff needed, their best deployment and the internal arrangement of the library. Assuming that these questions are settled in the light of a defined purpose, there remain innumerable day-to-day operations which give rise to a continuing variety of questions which in turn demand decisions. Such are problems of reservation policy, the location and withdrawal of books from stock, the role within a system of branch libraries, and the nature of the library's participation in co-operative schemes. The library needs to be a completely integrated organisation, which it cannot be unless purpose permeates every aspect of its activities. A clearly defined purpose, understood, offers criteria in the light of which every kind of decision demanded of the librarian can be determined. Lack of purpose will result in contradictory decisions, the subjection of the librarian to every kind of pressure, and the adoption of expediency as the customary solution to all problems.

Perhaps the most significant justification for accepting the need for purpose is the desirability that librarians, as professional workers, should acquire a sense of worthwhileness concerning their work. Purpose provides the inspiration for the quality of dedication essential to the librarian if he is to be fully effective. Without purpose the librarian remains a technician, his satisfactions limited to what may be gained from skill in practical operations; he is without commitment and cannot be regarded as equipped to formulate and direct policy.

Purpose as applied to libraries is variously understood to embrace function, objectives and (sometimes) uses. For my part I prefer to understand purpose as applying to libraries in general, objectives as applying to particular libraries and function as applying to the mode in which libraries operate, *ie* as mechanisms or instruments. To select the particular uses of libraries as equivalent to their purpose appears to substitute ways in which purpose is achieved for purpose itself. From this point of view, the question, ' Should recreation be a purpose for libraries?' needs to be rephrased as, ' Should recreation be considered a use appropriate to the purpose of libraries?'. The point of these distinctions is to avoid the temptation of transposing the terms so that in developing a thesis, the premises on which it is based are either deliberately or unconsciously modified. Such emphasis on terms would not be necessary but for the fact that much which has been said on the subject of the aims and purposes of libraries is confusing simply because the terms used have been switched about indiscriminately.

How is the problem of assigning purpose to libraries to be approached? The possibility of doing so arises from the functional characteristics of the library. The library operates to acquire and store books and printed material, and to organise the material in such ways as to enable any of it to be readily available to users. The physical limitations of storage impose the necessity for selection and rejection of material. Thus the range and nature of the material to be made available can be controlled. As to users, they too can be controlled by imposing conditions of eligibility. By manipulation of bookstocks and access thereto, the authority controlling the resources needed to maintain the library can impose whatever objectives it considers desirable. The authorities with the necessary resources may be private individuals, limited liability corporations, professional groups, institutions, associations of people combining for particular ends and the community at large. As we live in a pluralistic society, that is to say, one in which there exist simultaneously innumerable diverse interests and ideologies, it is inevitable that the objectives set for libraries will vary accordingly. Thus a homogeneous set of objectives, to which all libraries could conform, is not possible.

Are we to conclude then that the concept of a purpose embracing libraries in general is nullified by the circumstances in which, in particular, they operate? If, however, we observe the distinction between the purpose of libraries in general and the objectives of particular libraries, the possibility that one could be compatible with the other is not necessarily ruled out. Within a national economy, for example, there prevails a great diversity of economic activities, each one pursuing its own objectives, yet each nevertheless, compatible with the needs of the economy as a whole. There will be of course, certain conditions in which the objectives of some economic activities may not be so compatible. The exceptions however, do not preclude the possibility of attaining a wide measure of unity with diversity.

If a unifying purpose cannot be sought within the objectives of individual libraries, it can only be found within a wider context. Such a context could be the community or the national state, but we know that these pursue divergent objectives and that their libraries are likely to be conditioned accordingly. The only context which is not competitive with any other is society itself, *ie* the whole structure, which includes all human relationships. These relationships, which are integral with the nature of man, are the *raison d'être* of society, and are themselves completely dependent upon man's ability to develop processes and systems of communication. As Professor J Z Young, in a Reith Lecture, has said, ' We are now beginning to understand the importance of communication itself as a human activity . . . What I hope to show is that proper use of communication has been the chief secret of success of human societies in the past, and that it will certainly be so both in the immediate and more distant future . . . It is only by proper communication that human societies retain the adherence of their members.'[2]

Books constitute one process of communication, and libraries, whose function is to store and make them available, form part of the total system of communication. To this extent then, all libraries operate with one purpose; they all exist to facilitate the process of communication. Obvious as this may appear, it is not a trivial role for libraries to play. Norbert Weiner places that role in its correct perspective when he says, ' We have seen that communication is the cement of society, and that those who have made the clear maintenance of channels of communication their business are those who have most to do with the continued existence or fall of our civilisation.'[3] Even more explicit about the libraries' role is Herman H Fussler: 'A distinguishing feature of modern culture or non-primitive civilisation is its dependence on the written word as the principle device through which, (1) the knowledge of our time is recorded for the future, (2) the state of contemporary knowledge and ideas is communicated, and (3) the knowledge of the past becomes available to contemporary man. If this is true, or even approximately true, the critical role of the library in relation to the advance and to the preservation of modern civilisation becomes obvious, for the library is the major social organisation that systematically acquires, organises and preserves, that makes the activities described above possible and its role is a major one in connection with the communication of contemporary knowledge as well.'[4]

Accepting that libraries in general have an essential purpose in their role as part of the overall system of communication, one may yet argue that this purpose is so generalised that other processes of communication could supplant, or be more effective than libraries. Can we define the libraries' purpose more specifically, so as to distinguish it from that of other similar processes? The feature which distinguishes the various processes of communication is the medium which is used in each case. For libraries it is the book and the book possesses characteristics which give it an unique role among the media of communication. The so called mass-media, newspapers, radio, television and the cinema are, for economic reasons, aimed at very large audiences. The mass-media are thus obliged to confine expression to broadly accepted modes of thought and feeling. The book, however, is economically viable when aimed at infinitely smaller audiences; and is free, not only to express the least widely acceptable modes of thought and feeling, but can do so in depth. The library, as an institution whose principal medium is the book, offers the opportunity of representing the greatest variety of ideas and modes of thought and feeling, however microscopically these may be present in contemporary culture. The book is also distinguished by its facility for recall and recapitulation, and the greater intellectual effort it demands of the user. The latter needs to translate from the oral to the written language symbol. For the most part the mass-media rely on the oral language or the directly visual.

We may say then that the purpose of libraries is one of communication, but of a qualitatively different kind from that of most other such systems. This qualitative difference gives to the purpose of libraries its particular social significance. In general we may say that whereas the mass-media feeds the forces of inertia in society, libraries feed the forces making for change and adaptation. It does not follow that the mass-media make no contribution to change. A minority point of view may reach a threshold of acceptability within a community, which is sufficiently viable economically for the mass-media to give it expression; the mass-media may then take it up and actually assist in converting the minority view into a majority one. But, the minority view is likely, in the first instance, to have been nurtured and tended through books and the libraries which have provided the larger part of the audience for them.

What we have said about the purpose of libraries in general could as well have been said of the book industry, from author to retail distributor. The book industry, however, although vital in this process of communication, is precluded from achieving the maximum potential of the purpose which it serves in two ways; it is not specially concerned with the conservation and retrieval of books nor is it concerned with extending the audience for books beyond economic limits. Society has invented the mechanism of the library precisely in order that the process of communication, of which the book is the medium, shall achieve its full potential. In the next chapter I describe how the library functions to fulfil this purpose—' It (the library) has a technical, a social and an economic function. Its technical function has been likened to that of a computer. It is a storage and retrieval mechanism. It stores all the knowledge and thought and the records of experience of past and present generations—it is the social memory. By a variety of devices it retrieves and makes available whatever is wanted from the social memory, as and when required. The capacity of its storage and the rapidity of its retrieval facility are the criteria of its technical efficiency. The social role however, goes beyond serving the social memory. It is also a part of the total system of communication . . A widely diffused system of libraries within the community not only offers the possibility of extending the range of audiences for the book, but can assure unrestricted access to the great diversity of ideas and thought which is stimulated by the everchanging problems arising from the man-made and natural environment . . . In this sense the range of books available and the degree of accessibility afforded to them are a measure of the social efficiency of the library. Almost by definition, the library possesses also an economic function. By enabling single copies of books to be used by more than one reader it not only extends the potential audience for the book, but it reduces the total resources required to meet the reading needs of the community.' The purpose of libraries in general therefore, is to extend to its potential limits the audience for that process of communication whose medium is books and the printed word. It does so by conserving and organising these as the social memory, and by affording effective and unrestricted access to them.

Not all types of library pursue objectives which are fully compatible with the purpose of libraries in general. Those, for example, which are established to propagate a particular point of view, or those in which the book stocks are restricted as the result of coercive forces, whether intellectual or political, cannot be regarded as fully compatible. Fortunately, the effect of books on individual readers is so unpredictable that such libraries are unlikely to be entirely successful in achieving their objectives. Special and academic libraries of all kinds pursue objectives which may involve limiting the range of books available, or the extent of their readerships, but they do so in order to offer more effective accessibility to groups of readers whose interests and activities are closely related to the fields of literature represented in such libraries. Thus, their objectives in no way negate the overall purpose of libraries. Similarly national libraries, whose principal objective is, commonly, the preservation of books, must impose conditions which limit their use to readers who can be safely entrusted to use them. To do otherwise would negate a vital aspect of the overall purpose, namely, the preservation and conservation of books. The many different objectives which, individually, a great variety of libraries pursue, can be regarded therefore as fully compatible with the overall purpose of libraries, although in particular, their objectives may require more emphasis to be placed on some aspects of that purpose than on others. It follows also that there can be a common set of principles underlying the practice of librarianship in all its applications.

I have attempted to show that, with a few exceptions, the great variety of types of libraries can be regarded as serving a common unifying purpose. This purpose is necessarily of a general character, but it does possess a degree of social significance of the highest order, and one which only the invention of the library idea has made possible. A variety of special, academic and national libraries will, taken together, offer to a community which is well provided with them a stock of books covering a considerable range of literature. These libraries rarely function other than as independent units, each attracting its own exclusive groups of readers, so that their book stocks are unlikely to extend to the entire range of literature currently available. Even were this not so, their readers will have little opportunity of access to literature beyond the scope of the library unit to which, as readers, they are allied. More importantly, these libraries will not cater for the many potential readers in the community who do not qualify to use them.

The book-based process of communication cannot be fully exploited, therefore, unless another type of library is well distributed within a community. Such a library will need to place emphasis on two aspects of the overall purpose. It will facilitate access to the whole range of literature, and will ensure that every member of the community who cares to do so enjoys the right to that access. The kind of library which is capable of fulfilling these requirements is the public library, whose resources are controlled by an authority responsible only to the community at large. The way in which libraries contribute to their overall purpose is through the objectives which are set for them, and it is around these that the management and structuring of the libraries has to be designed. For types of libraries other than public libraries, this is seldom a problem, but lacking accepted pre-stated objectives and an awareness of their relationship with the book-based process of communication and its potentialities, public libraries have had a variety of objectives ascribed to them.

As I have said, the aspects of the overall library purpose which it is the role of the public library to pursue lie in affording unrestricted access to the whole range of literature. To sustain this role, the public library is faced with the problem arising from its limited book stock, which can only be solved through systems of co-operation with other libraries. An organisation in which all libraries, including the public library, are fully integrated on a co-operative basis is essential to the fulfilment of the overall purpose. It follows also that the internal organisation of the public library must be so arranged that guidance to readers is available not only to its own book stock but to those books beyond its scope. The problem remains however, as to what objectives are to be set for forming and controlling its own book stock, and for designing its organisation so as to minimise demands upon co-operative systems. The solution should neither side-step nor limit the library's contribution to the overall purpose.

A review of the principal solutions to the problem which have been put forward from time to time may help subsequently, to project our own conclusions in a clearer light. One view which is very pervasive is that the principal objective of the public library is ' educational '.

The educational objective: At once we are faced with the difficulty of the meaning we attach to ' educational '. If it is understood in its widest sense as perhaps, enlightenment, and especially if it were qualified by the condition that for readers it was entirely self-sought, we might consider it acceptable. It tends, however, to be used in an exclusive sense which restricts the kinds of books considered acceptable for the book stock. As a number of writers have pointed out, education is one of the ways in which society attempts to mould thought and behaviour. Professor Meredith, for example says, ' The child on entering school enters on a life of organisation . . . Unfortunately the better the organisation the less well-equipped he is on leaving school.'[5] He further says, ' For reading is a process of self-discovery, as well as a pathway to knowledge . . . The reader can re-organise his mind at his own pace and on his own terms.' Professor de Vleeschauwr goes even further, boldly stating that the library is the corrective of the school.'[6] Erich Fromm defines the social role of education as being ' to qualify the individual to function in the role he is to play later on in society; to mould the character in such a way that it approximates the social character, that his desires coincide with the necessities of his social role.'[7] In our view, an objective which implicitly involves an attempt to mould the reader is not consistent with the role of the public library, so that we cannot accept that education should be its principal objective.

The social objective: There are a number of objectives which might be grouped under the heading of the social objective. These too imply the use of the public library to mould or control its readership for some state or community aim. In some national systems the public library is expected to foster a national policy either of a political character, or a form of homogeneity desired by exclusive groups of citizens. To cite current examples we have only to refer to communist states or the so called 'American way of life '. A similar objective is one which aims to foster ' democracy ', and which will almost certainly mean a particular concept of democracy. None of these kinds of objectives appear to do other than mis-use the library and to thwart its potentialities. There are more innocuous community aims which, under some conditions cannot be unduly criticised from our point of view. One such is the encouragement of literacy which in itself can lead to more extensive use of the library; nevertheless one would want to make the proviso that the aim should not be allowed for overlong to restrict readers' access to the wider realms of literature.

The demand objective: An often criticised objective is one which may be described as the ' demand objective '. In other words, ' give people what they want '. One could go along with this if the limited book stock of the library could cope. The practical outcome, however, is likely to involve sacrificing groups of readers with the more microscopic interests to the more vociferous ' big battalions ' among the readership. As I hope to have shown, it is one of the more vital of the library's obligations to ensure that these microscopic interests in society are adequately allowed for in the book stock. The demand objective, which implies that those books most called for should receive priority, is likely to result in inequality of opportunity within the readership.

The established truth objective: There is a somewhat naive view, which must be mentioned, which is expressed by Leon Carnovsky: ' What I am arguing for is a librarian whose predelictions are for established truths and who then bases his book selection upon these truths . . . In connection with religion . . . I should say that since virtually all faiths aim at the fundamental religious principles of justice, morality, mercy, they all deserve representation . . . the principle of wide representation . . . should never be applied to justify the equal provision of established truths and their denials.'[8] Carnovsky concludes his essay on book selection by throwing down a challenge to librarians —' which shall we be, politicians or statesmen?'.

Surely it is by challenging established truths that new truths are discovered. The role of the public library does not oblige the librarian to be either a politician or a statesman, although, of course, an understanding of the ways in which such people operate can be of inestimable value to the public librarian.

The recreational or amenity objective: Outside professional circles, it is not uncommon for the public library to be seen as primarily a recreational or amenity service. In fact, this is the category in which the Association of Municipal Corporations normally places the public library. This is an example of the error which confuses a possible use with a principal objective of the library. Thereby, other types of use are reduced in status and the significant role of the library is completely missed. It is quite a different matter when this particular use is catered for in the light of the same principle of selection as are all other uses—for it is not then given the priority or status of an objective.

Standards objective: One school of thought considers that standards for selection are properly objectives for the library. Generally this demand for standards in selection applies to the fields of imaginative literature, but, if it is seen as a principal objective, it may well be at the expense of other fields of literature where relevance is a more appropriate criterion. The use of standards in selection is more properly aligned with the librarian's function as a guide to literature. In this sense it is not in conflict with the role of the library, providing that the standards are not imposed upon the readership. As C S Lewis once said, ' We must never assume that we know exactly what is happening when anyone else reads a book '. To assume otherwise is to fall into the fallacy underlying Carnovsky's objective of supporting ' established truths '.

I have not attempted to deal fully with these views of the library's objectives, but only sufficiently to indicate that in one way or another they either limit the readership, or, more commonly, aim to use the library to direct or mould the reader towards some desired ends which are not necessarily the ends which the reader himself desires or might discover for himself.

The theme of this paper has been to relate the purpose of libraries in general to a relatively permanent concept. Purpose is sought in the nature of the library's role within the social structure and from which it cannot be considered apart. Society cannot function without systems of communication. Libraries form part of the book-based process of communication, which is inherently different to any other, and this difference gives them a particular and high social significance. There are various types of libraries, and by and large they all serve this unifying purpose, but the public library is needed to exploit the full potential of the book-based process of communication. It can do so because it has the capability of ensuring that all sections of the community can gain unrestricted access to the widest range of literature. By exercising this capability as effectively as resources will permit, the public library is the one process of communication which seeks neither to exploit, control or mould. It affords the opportunity to the individual to engage in the process of self-discovery and to re-organise himself. By ensuring that its bookstock reflects all trends of contemporary ideas and views, and especially those which are only just emerging into articulation, it fosters the possibility of the continued adaptation of man and society to changing needs and circumstance. It accepts as fact the plurality of society, and declines to be pressurised into any kind of homogeneity. In plain words it stands for the freedom and autonomy of the individual in the sense conveyed by Sapir[9] when he refers to 'the fundamental intent and direction of every personality organisation'.

I would describe its principal objective as the 'open-ended' objective. As to the quality of life and the cultural standards which books may enrich, yes, these too it can foster, but not at the expense of the freedom of the individual to find his own way. Without freedom, the quality of life cannot develop. The freedom which the library stands for thwarts the ever present pressures for conformity.

For practical purposes we can summarise the requirements of the open-ended objective as:

a) The subject of the library is the people who use it, so that the assessment of their needs and interests is paramount.

b) The book stock must reflect the changing interests of its readers, and it must provide sufficient material to sustain and intensify interests which are the subject of very small demand, even at the expense of material which attracts the heaviest demand.

c) Its staff must be organised to provide readers with guidance to the 'map of literature' and not merely to the 'map of the library's own book stock'. In the guidance function the library will seek to indicate what is relevant to the reader's interest, and what may be judged to be the best of its kind, but it will leave the reader to decide what he considers relevant and what he considers best.

d) It must seek every possibility of gaining access for its readers to all that material which for good reasons is beyond the scope of the library's own book stock.

e) It will initiate and foster activities which extend the influence of the library within the community as its natural and freely available resources centre for the cultural, intellectual and informational needs which the book and its related media can meet.

There is a Japanese proverb which runs: 'A nail that sticks up above the others, invites the hammer'. That represents the philosophy, which above all, it is the purpose of the public library to destroy.

REFERENCES

1 McIver, R M: *Community*. 1924.

2 Young, J Z: *Doubt and certainty in science*. Reith Lecture, 1951.

3 Weiner, Norbert: *The human use of human beings*. Eyre & Spottiswoode, 1950.

4 Fussler, Herman H *in* Fussler, H H and Simon, J L : *Patterns in the use of books in large research libraries.* University of Chicago Library, 1961.

5 Meredith, Patrick : *Learning, remembering and knowing.* EUP, 1961.

6. de Vleeschauver, H J : ' Library deontology '. *Mousaion* (Univ of South Africa), nos 48 to 51.

7 Fromm, Erich : *Fear of freedom.* Routledge, 1960.

8 Carnovsky, L *in* Wilson, Louis R *(ed)*: *The practice of book selection.* Univ of Chicago Press, 1949.

9 Sapir, Edward : *Culture, language and personality: selected essays edited by David G Mandelbaum.* University of California Press, Berkeley and Los Angeles, 1970.

12: *Library developments affecting the book trade*

PERHAPS at no other time have there been so many influences and developments at work affecting the practice of librarianship and the role of the library in the community. To predict the impact of these in specific terms, even in the short run, would be difficult if not impossible, and to pretend to be able to do so would betray a degree of arrogance with which I should prefer not to be charged. Nevertheless, one may venture to distinguish a number of developments of a general or technical character which may have significance and, rather less surely, to indicate some of their possibilities.

There are, I am sure, a number of subtle and complex relationships between the roles of the book industry and the library which have not, regrettably, been adequately explored. Our ignorance of these leads too often to over-simplified judgments about them. We are accustomed to understand the library in terms of the uses made of it by individuals and groups, or of the various motivations of people for its use. So we see certain economists, for example, straying into the field of ethics and attempting to justify one particular use or motive for use as against others, not on economic but on moral grounds. To see the library in those terms is to rely upon constantly changing assumptions and intellectual fashion. Increasingly, I think, the library will be seen in more stable and permanent terms, which afford a better basis for understanding its role in the community, and in particular its relationships with the book industry.

The library can be seen as a social invention, as indeed is the ' book '. It has a technical, a social and an economic function. Its technical function has been likened to that of the computer. It is a storage and retrieval mechanism. It stores all the knowledge and thought and the records of experience of past and present generations—it is the social memory. By a variety of devices it retrieves and makes available whatever is wanted from the memory, as and when required. The capacity of its storage and the rapidity of its retrieval facility are the criteria of its technical efficiency.

The social role however goes beyond serving as the social memory. It is also a part of the total system of communication. Whereas most means of communication demand large financial resources, depend upon securing enormous audiences, and so tend to foster widely accepted ideas and attitudes, the ' book ' is economically viable, even in current conditions, with infinitely smaller audiences. The book industry therefore, can cater profitably for a wide range of minority ideas and attitudes. A widely diffused system of libraries within the community not only offers the possibility of extending the range of audiences for the book, but can guarantee unrestricted access to the great diversity of ideas and thought which are stimulated by the ever changing problems arising from the man-made and the natural environment. The successful solutions which enable society to adapt itself to its problems invariably emerge from a minority level. The book and the freedom of accessibility to it afforded by the library are, therefore, vital elements in the system of communication if an ' open ' society is to survive. In this sense the range of books available and the degree of accessibility afforded to them is a measure of the social efficiency of the library. In this area the roles of the book industry and the library are interdependent, and they each have an interest in the success and efficiency of the other.

Almost by definition the library possesses an economic function. By enabling single books to be used by more than one reader it reduces the cost of reading to the individual, and, more significantly, it reduces the total resources needed to meet the reading needs of the community. This aspect of the library's functions appears to suggest a basis of conflict between the book industry and the library. It is, perhaps, too readily assumed that increase in the multiple use of books must involve a decrease in their purchase and, conversely, that a decrease in multiple use would ensure that more books would be purchased. Again we encounter another area in which research has been almost non-existent, and which, if it had been undertaken, would almost certainly reveal that the situation was much more complex than a simple cause and effect reasoning would imply. In spite of the lack of research on the subject of the economics of reading, it is possible to think of a number of factors which suggest that the relationship between the borrowing and buying of books is more one of interdependence than of conflict.

A number of investigations have been made into the reading habits of people, and wherever these have touched upon the relationship between borrowing and buying of books they have confirmed the thesis that those who borrow most tend to buy most. This is supported by commonsense. One may reasonably assume that those who borrow most are likely to be inveterate readers, are likely to have a greater love of books for their own sake, than those who borrow least. Their potential for buying is likely therefore to be the greater. Although the increase in total multiple use of books may not have been accompanied by a directly proportionate increase in the buying of books, there is little doubt that the buying of books has in fact increased at the same time.

An analogy for this relationship might be seen in the behaviour of a simple gas-flame as the supply of gas is raised or lowered. The flame is seen to consist of an outer yellow portion and an inner blue portion. If the gas supply is increased, both portions of the flame increase in size; when the gas supply is reduced both portions are correspondingly reduced. We might press the analogy a little further. Having seen that the larger yellow portion of the flame corresponds to the multiple use of books and that the inner blue portion corresponds to the buying of books we may wonder to what the gas supply corresponds. I suggest it could correspond to the significance of reading to the individual consumer of books. As reading becomes more significant to the individual and the community, both multiple use and buying increase and conversely so. I think we might find that the buying of books is more directly related to expenditure on other needs than it is to the availability of borrowing facilities. The more efficiently the library meets readers' needs, the more each reader comes to appreciate the value and utility of books in his personal life, and as a result the likelihood is that the relative significance of books within the scale of his other needs will increase. On the other hand, a loss of efficiency and a restriction on multiple use within the library is likely to reduce the significance of reading and to lead to less buying of books. The power of radio and television is very much a factor of their ever ready availability. So too with books and reading. All investigations into reading habits confirm that when books are part of the accepted background of life, reading potential is high. Availability and accessibility are important factors in the level of significance attached to reading. A widespread system of libraries in the community makes a considerable contribution to this end. Would this positive relationship between the multiple use and the buying of books suggest that more books might be sold if bookshops were located in the library? In our universities, bookshops are found located near the focal point of learning, the library. Should we try municipal bookshops in the local library, or will some enterprising bookseller overcome all the difficulties and rent space in some new central municipal library, yet to be built?

The markets or audiences which the book industry and the library respectively seek to cater for clearly overlap, but there exist essential differences between them. Although the book industry to an extent greater than any other does meet demands for its product which are not commercially viable, its ability to do this is limited and becomes increasingly so. The library in its social role seeks out all reading needs, whether they are commercially viable or not. Thereby, the library not only reveals gaps in the available literature, but, by consolidating such minority needs in national terms creates a marginal demand which may suffice to justify commercial production. The multiple use and freedom of accessibility which the library offers also serves to stimulate the growth of particular reading interests, which in turn increases the range of books acceptable to the commercial market. Where the gaps in the literature are such as cannot be bridged commercially, the library is justified in subsidising the cost of production. This is already done to a certain extent. It would be interesting to know what proportion of the total annual output of book titles is commercially self-supporting and of those that are not, how they came to be financed. I think the library could do more in contributing to the cost of production to ensure that books achieve publication in fields where suitable books are scarce. In this connection both the book industry and the library tend to think along the lines of particular books which have gone out of print. Useful as it undoubtedly is to resurrect valuable material, it could be no less useful to induce publication of new material where suitable material does not exist.

To complete our survey of the economic interplay of the library and the book industry I would draw attention to what I can only describe as a mental blockage common to people engaged in both. One frequently hears plaintive arguments to the effect that the price of books is not viewed by the potential consumer in the same light as he may view the other things he wants or does. It is said, for example, that the price of a book is certainly less than the price of an evening at the theatre and, whereas the consumer thinks nothing of the latter, he is much more resistant to the former. Apart from the invalidity of the comparison, it seems to me to be based on a false idea of the relation of readers to books. It may be understandable that people in the book industry and librarians and others concerned with books professionally should think of reading in terms of its physical units, namely individual books. I should say that a great deal of reading is not thought of in these terms by regular readers. To the reader, a great deal of his reading is a continuous activity. It is not necessarily seen as a series of isolated events in the form of particular books. From his total reading activity the number of individual books which make an impact equivalent to an ' event ' will be small. Reading as an habitual activity is more like a ciné-film, composed it is true of a series of discrete units, but affording the illusion of continuity. In a number of ways it is an extension of conversation and discussion, where particular conversations merge into a continuum and are frequently lost in memory, as distinct pieces of experience.

The habitual reader may therefore see the cost of books not so much in terms of the prices of a few individual books a year, but rather in terms of the cost of maintaining his continuous reading activity. He needs to read many books in order to determine which ones are significant enough for him to want to possess them. Currently such a reader might find that it would cost him anything from £50 to £200 a year to maintain his reading activity. This puts his attitude to the purchase of books in a different light. Hence also the economic basis for the invention of the library, and perhaps its role as the greatest free sampling adjunct available to any industry. All of us concerned with books professionally might consider whether the availability of the facility for continuous reading is at least as important to the individual reader as the availability of particular titles.

I have devoted some time to the role of the library, because if two parties to a discussion are to produce fruitful results it is as well for them to know what the other is about. I have probably in my innocence strayed too far into the realm of the economic interplay of the library and the book industry, but I was tempted to do this because here it seemed was the likely source of differences, and if they exist I think it is important to the discussion that we should ascertain whether they are of a fundamental or of a complementary character. The evidence is that there is no serious basis for conflict, but rather that the activities of both are complementary and interdependent. This being the case any development affecting the one must be of interest to the other.

Developments which are likely to affect the libraries' selection of stock will consist of those of a general character affecting the librarian's attitude to his stock and those of a specific technical character affecting his methods of selection.

There is a variety of factors at work which seem to be leading towards similar ends. The Public Libraries Act, and other activities of government in relation to libraries such as the National Lending Library for Science & Technology, indicate a greater appreciation of the role of libraries at national level. There is pressure for the extension and improvement of facilities for higher education, and the parallel trend for more sophisticated professional training. In the municipal field the larger library system will certainly become the typical unit. The national necessity for modernising our industries and institutions may be about to ' bite ' local government, and it is unlikely that libraries will remain immune.

National recognition of the library's role and the extension of higher education will substantially increase the demand upon the library's resources. Clearly, more money will be spent on books, although possibly not to the extent that is necessary because of the competition among many services for a greater proportion of public funds. The additional expenditure may not be enough seriously to affect the library's share of the total turnover of the book trade. It is likely however to alter the pattern of book buying in that a greater range of less popular books will be purchased. In turn the library's contribution in stimulating the publication of books which are barely viable commercially will be greater, off-setting to some extent the effects of the current trend for the minimum economic print run to increase. The extension of higher education, the urge for modernisation and the improved levels of professional training will stimulate the growth of a more widely discriminating readership in the community. All the influences I have mentioned, together with the decline in quality levels of agencies such as television, should reinforce the continuing expansion in the use of the library. Concurrently there should be an increase in the significance of reading resulting, if relative affluence continues, in an expanding market for books.

It is difficult to relate such general influences directly to the librarian's actual selection of stock, which is more likely to be modified by technical and professional developments. The pressures from a more demanding and discriminating readership may cause librarians to change their emphasis in due course from methodology to bibliographical know-how and guidance. The importance of bibliographical aids is indicated by the success of the *British national bibliography,* but we are already aware that the range of available aids is inadequate to meet even current requirements.

The concentration of libraries into larger units which will follow local government reorganisation is likely to stimulate the growth of specialisation in subject bibliography and in subject stock provision. Book selection will be distributed over a greater number of professional staff, and the senior librarian with increased administrative responsibilities will tend to draw away from direct personal selection, and will need, in consequence, to develop methods of coordinating and controlling his overall stock provision. We may see develop a conception of the public library as a coordinated series of special libraries, bringing the public librarian and the specialist librarian closer in outlook. The librarian's attitude to his stock may then shift towards a more deliberate building up of the stock, with less emphasis being placed on the need to concentrate on the immediate flood of new general literature. More time will be devoted to sifting out the new material in rela tion to a more detailed analysis of stock and reader requirements, and in accordance with a more thought-out bibliographical pattern.

The kind of information required about readers and stock will become more readily available as access to computer facilities improves. There is little doubt that the computer will have a major impact on all departments of local government, not least in libraries. The computer will enable the library to reduce the level of its routine work for example in issue control, overdue and similar procedures; it will probably revolutionise the catalogue procedures, and thus release staff for the intensified bibliographical functions of the library. More significantly however, it will afford just the facilities needed to provide the detailed analysis of stock and readers which is rarely possible at the present time. On the basis of such information the librarian will be able to develop a systematic approach to book provision in place of the empirical approach which hitherto he has been obliged to adopt. The problem of the chief librarian in controlling a group of subject librarians will also be simplified.

These developments will also ' tie in ' with the inevitable growth of more sophisticated forms of cooperation between libraries. The combination of increased cooperation and the improved information about books and readers, if extended to the book industry, may prove to be invaluable in assessing market possibilities as well. One of the mildly surprising results of the great extension in library cooperative schemes which has occurred in recent years is that, in spite of a general increase in book funds, interlibrary loans continue to mount rapidly. Clearly, improvements in availability serve to stimulate demand, and we can expect the trend to continue.

The setting up of the regional councils proposed in the Public Libraries Act is likely to lead to a close examination of interlending principles, together with the possibilities of central storage of books. Improvement in the level of information about books and readers may lead to more adequate criteria being evolved for the determination of such questions as whether a book should be borrowed from other library sources, or whether it should be purchased, and which of a number of libraries should hold copies. We may thus see librarians' obligations to stock books under subject-specialisation schemes considerably extended. With these and the other developments referred to as possibilities, the art of book selection may reach such a level of complexity that its practitioners may even turn to science for assistance!

Can we indicate ways in which the book-industry may help the librarian as his book selection task becomes more complex, as indeed I think we can predict with some certainty that it will?

The librarian will look for improved bibliographical information; will be grateful for any cooperation received in the production of improved bibliographical tools. Already booksellers and publishers are showing willingness in these directions. Would the industry consider the idea of setting up 'book centres' in three or four major cities including London, on the lines of the Design Centre? Some trades do set up 'information shops' as well as selling shops. I visualise a book centre displaying for periods of, say, not less than 6 months, one copy of every new publication, and staffed on a small scale by thoroughly well-trained assistants, who would be in a position to deal with inquiries about current books, and able to give addresses of local bookshops where they may be bought. Could the National Book League undertake such a project? One sees possibilities of periodically arranged special displays incorporating copies of every title in print on one particular subject. Such a centre would of course be open to the general public, but could be of particular value to librarians and others concerned with institutional buying in enabling them to see at first hand a range of new books published over a fair period. The National Book League does already function in this way, but not, I think, as comprehensively as I envisage.

Would the industry consider more adequate machinery than now exists to foster the publication of out of print books? Would the industry welcome information organised by libraries on a national scale concerning subject fields in which suitable books are scarce, and endeavour to stimulate the publication of such books among its membership!

And a final question, are there *good* books which publishers have to reject on economic grounds? If there are, could the principle of subscription prior to publication be extended and support from libraries sought to make publication possible? I am sure many librarians would feel justified in paying a higher price than the normal commercial price for such books.

Index